THE WORLD'S 100 GREATEST INVENTIONS THAT WEIGH LESS THAN 16 OUNCES

A whimsical, tongue-in-cheek look at some everyday items.

D. L. Thomas

2nd Edition

4

TABLE OF CONTENTS

THINGS YOU NEED TO KNOW

1. If item is listed as plural, it is less than 16 oz. if singular.
2. Items in categories are alphabetical. Not by value or use.
3. Items are less than 16 oz. in their basic configuration but they may be more in other applications or sophistications.
4. Some items, such as aluminum foil, are many square feet before weighing 16 ounces. They are normally used in much smaller pieces.
5. Names of inventors are accurate as far as is known. The veracity of the remainder is questionable.
6. Items are manufactured or man-made. No food or drink.

4

NUMERICAL LIST

4

4

<u>ALPHABETICAL LIST</u>

4

Kitchen & dining items

1. Aluminum foil

Aluminum foil is the brainchild of Danish chemist Hans Christian Oersted. He invented it way back in 1825. It was very expensive until 1889 when Charles Martin Hall developed an inexpensive way to refine the alum, which comes from a rock named bauxite. It is the basic material of aluminum, or aluminium as some people call it. Mr. Hall received a patent on it April 2, 1854. He founded the Aluminum Company of America (ALCOA). Aluminum foil production started about 1910. Now it is best known as being a very thin, less than .02mm, sheet of light weight metal used to wrap leftover food you can store in your refrigerator until it gets pushed to the rear and turns rotten because you can't see what's inside it. One of the definitions of 'foil' is 'to prevent'. We could assume that if we wrap the leftovers in foil they will be prevented from spoiling. They're not.

2. Bottle caps

We have all popped the top off a few cans in our life. Whether those cans contained a soft drink or a beer is immaterial. This discussion is about that small metal object atop the bottle, the bottle cap. The bottle cap, or the crown cap as it is known, was the invention of William Painter of Baltimore, Maryland in 1892. Mr. Painter was born in Ireland and emigrated to the United States in 1859 at the age of twenty. He received U.S. patent #468,258 for his invention. It was a circular steel cap 26mm in diameter with 24 teeth encircling the edge. Mr. Painter collaborated with the manufacturers of glass bottles to standardize the bottle tops. Today there are 21 teeth encircling the edge. The reduction in the number of teeth may have been a concession to the bottle manufacturers. None of the participants in the negotiations are presently available to confirm or deny.

If you have ever tried to recap a European bottle with the cap from a U. S. bottle it won't fit. European caps are 28mm, not 26.

Mr. Painter founded Crown Cork and Seal Company to manufacture the caps. Today it is called Crown Holdings. It is one of the Fortune 500 Companies. Mr. Painter is a member of the Inventors Hall of Fame. He had 85 patents among them is the patent for the twist-off cap. The twist-off is made with a softer metal than the pry off. This permits the teeth to be pushed aside when the twist-off force is applied. The twist off caps have a PVC liner instead of cork, to better impede oxygen from leaking into the bottle.

3. Can opener (manual)

Peter Durand invented the tin can in 1810. When the food purveyors increased the amount of food they purveyed by putting it in the tin cans to preserve it, they immediately recognized the problem of accessing the food when a person was hungry enough to eat it. The engineers and inventors set to work finding an easy way to open those darn cans. The cans were of thicker tin than what is used today. It took until 1858 before Ezra Warner invented a can opener that could open them. It is unknown if the food in Durand's cans from 1810 was still edible when opened by Warner's can opener in 1858. Warner's can opener was used extensively until 1870 when William Lyman invented the rolling wheel cutter. It is basically the same design we use today.

4. Chopsticks

Indeterminate origin. Thousands of years old. They may possibly be a modification of the caveman's use of two sticks to remove his food from the fire. It can be easily explained how a person could hold two thinner sticks in one hand in a manner in which they would be able to hold on to morsels of food while swatting flies or something with the other hand. Chopsticks are difficult to use with soup as is the fork. That is why the spoon was invented, or you can hold the bowl up and slurp the soup out of the bowl.

5. Corkscrew

The calming effects of a glass of wine after a stressful day of labor were exacerbated for centuries by the frustrating task of removing the cork stopper placed in the bottle by the vintner to prevent air from getting into the bottle and spoiling his fine wine. However, the little cork stopper also prevented the thirsty worker from getting into the wine. There is no more deserving member of this list than the device necessary to remove the cork, the corkscrew. The first patent for a corkscrew was issued to the Reverend Samuel Henshall of England in 1795. He had Matthew Boulton of Birmingham England manufacture them. U.S. patents were issued to George Blanchard of New York in 1856 and to M. L. Byen, also of New York, in 1860. There was a French patent issued in 1828. All of them are variation of the basic design with enough variation to warrant a patent being issued. Historically, the inspiration for the corkscrew is considered to be the Gun Worm. The Gun Worm, also called the Bullet Screw, was used to remove bullets from guns when they misfired. It is unclear how the Reverend Henshall, a man of peace, knew so much about guns and gun worms in 1795. The little cork bottle stoppers are made from the bark of the cork oak tree. The tree grows primarily in the

Mediterranean region. The cork for a wine bottle weighs .2 of an ounce. It requires 80 of them to weigh 16 ounces. Cork has many uses other than stoppers for wine bottles. It is used as insulation in walk-in coolers and as flotation devices but most people these days are acquainted with it as a wine bottle plug.

6. Cups

This is a broad category with many different cups for many different uses. There are tin cups, coffee cups, egg cups, tea cups, measuring cups and athletic cups. (although they should not be in this category. Perhaps in personal items or recreation items, but not here). Cups have been in existence for thousands of years. Jesus, when praying in the garden of Gethsemane said 'take this cup from me'. He was speaking of an entirely different kind of cup but He did say 'cup'. There's a saying "in his cups" meaning the man has had too many alcoholic drinks. That is not heard much anymore because the majority of alcoholic beverages are not served in cups. They are served in bottles and cans and wine glasses appropriate for the vintage. There is one exception to the current lack of cups for alcohol. That is the 16 ounce plastic cups. They are the safety choice at swimming pools and the popular choice at country music concerts (especially the red ones) for fifty or more years.

7. Mason jars

John Landis Mason invented the Mason Jar in 1858. He was 26 years old when issued patent #22186. It was a glass jar with a patented tight fitting sealed lid for the preservation of foods. The Ball Brothers, Edmund, Frank, George, Lucas and William started manufacturing them in Buffalo, New York in 1884. They moved their manufacturing facility to Muncie, Indiana in 1887. At the height of their manufacturing process they were making 17 jars per second. Ball State University is on land donated by the Ball brothers. The factory and business were purchased by Newell Brands in 1993. Newell Brands is a conglomerate with $9.71 billion revenue. They own Rubbermaid, Coleman, Alert, Rival, Sunbeam, Crock-pot, Oster, Mr. Coffee and others. A one quart Mason Jar weighs 21 ounces. It would be too heavy to be in this book. However, the patent is for the lid, not the jar. The lid weighs 4 ounces.

8. Spoons

The spoon, or an item which serves the purpose of a spoon, has been helping us for eons. The word spoon is derived from the word *cochlea,* which means *shell.* A shell has a shape similar to a spoon but without the handle. As we progressed through the ages the shells acquired a handle. They stopped being shells and became items made of wood, glass, metal or plastic. Now we have different spoons designed to serve different purposes. There's the teaspoon and the table spoon. The table spoon is three times larger than the teaspoon. (That is not to say the tablespoon is three times *longer* than the teaspoon, it has three times the *capacity* of the teaspoon.) It is unclear why the normal table service includes a teaspoon instead of a tablespoon. One would think that since it is called 'table service', it would include a *table* spoon. In addition to the teaspoon and the table spoon, there's the soup spoon, the dessert spoon and the sugar spoon. The sugar spoon is smaller than the teaspoon. It is used to add sugar to your tea, although it is assumed you could use a teaspoon for that purpose. After all, it is called a *tea*spoon. The soup spoon was invented in the orient by a soup lover shortly after the invention of chopsticks. He was upset seeing others crudely picking up the soup bowl and slurping the soup. This does not mean you must use a soup spoon when having soup. You may use a tablespoon or a teaspoon whichever fits your mouth. There are other heavier spoons for mixing, stirring, baking* and basting. Most weigh less than 16 ounces, some don't.

> *For those that enjoy baking there is the measuring spoon. Measuring spoons are a group of spoons of small varying size used to add the proper amount of ingredients into your recipes on the theory that the final result will look as good as the picture shown and taste fabulous. Dreamer.

9. Straws (drinking)

I'm going to tell you something you already know. It's simple. You suck. That's how a straw works. As the centuries passed, man, and woman, became repulsed at using a reed to quench their thirst. The swamp water taste never seemed to leave. It was up to a man by the name of Marvin Stone to invent the modern drinking straw. He did so in 1888 and founded a Company cleverly named the Stone Straw Company to manufacture them. The Company is still in business today. His straws were wax coated paper tubes. Now, billions of straws are made annually of plastic. Too many of those straws find their way into the oceans and seas. It is unnecessary to have those straws in the water. If the sea creatures want a drink, they do not need a straw. They simply have to open their mouth.

10. Table service

This is your basic eating utensils, the knife and the fork. Let's review them in alphabetical order.

The Fork: The use of forks for dining was very rare until the 16th century. Catherine de Medici came from Italy to France in 1533 to marry King Henry II. She brought forks with her. Forks had arrived in Italy sometime between the 11th century when an illustration from Byzantium at that time shows men holding a two pronged dining instrument. Forks were considered by some as an insult to God. They were viewed as an abomination of sticking a foreign object into the food God has provided. A princess from a foreign nation who was in the Byzantine Empire in the 11th century used a utensil similar to a fork when dining. When she died of the plague it was thought to be God's punishment for her vanity. The first forks had long handles and two tines. They were used to hold large pieces of meat so it wouldn't twist and turn when carving. We still use similar utensils. There were no table forks in normal use. People stabbed food with their knife or used their fingers to grab it. Two kings of France, Henry III and Louis XIV, wouldn't allow pointed knives at their table. All knives had to have rounded tips. An Englishman, Thomas Coryate brought forks to England about 1611. He had acquired them in his travels to Italy. They were not well received at the time. They were thought to be an effeminate affectation. Over time forks began to be used by the wealthy. They were quite expensive and vanity and snobbery were reasons they were used by the upper class. The wealthy in Spain also used forks in the 16th century. It is said that Governor Winthrop of

Massachusetts had the only fork in America in 1630. The governor had brought it with him from England. Forks at the time had two tines. Forks with 3 and 4 tines began to appear about 1700. The standard is now four tines. Forks did not become part of the usual table service until the 18th century. Even as late as 1795 some English sailors would not use them thinking they were effeminate.

The Knife: This refers to the table knife as this the table service item. Other knives of he honed edge variety are reviewed in the Tools and Hardware category. The table knife as we know it is a relative newcomer to our dining experience. Knives have been used for eating since man first fashioned them from a sharp stone or piece of shale. Knives became weapons as well as eating utensils. Those used as weapons were normally larger and sharper than the table knife. They had sharp points to stab pieces of meat or something. In the 1630's King Louis XIII of France banned the use of pointed knives at the table as he dined with friends. He decreed the tips of the knives must be blunted. He was aware of what happened to Julius Caesar at the hands of friends. (et tu Brute). His son, Louis XIV, having learned from his father, decreed the same thing in 1669. Since then, the table knife has become a flat blade with a rounded tip and not nearly as threatening in appearance. The edge remains somewhat sharpened but incapable of cutting tough foods. The wide blade is used to spread butter, jelly and preserves. Peanut butter and jelly sandwiches would be impossible without this invention. There would be a terrible result from such an incident. Millions of school children would not have anything in their lunch box. Another advantage of this item is you don't need some special kind of knife to cut the p.b. & j. across the corners diagonally, the preferred choice of children everywhere. The edge is sharp enough for that purpose.

11. Tin can

Those soup lovers using the spoon have only to open a can using a can opener, empty the contents into a bowl or pan, heat until hot and enjoy. Before the invention of the tin can, food couldn't be preserved for more than a few days. The tin can is the invention of Peter Durand as mentioned earlier. He invented it in 1810. The first tin cans manufactured commercially were in 1813. They were of thicker tin than what is now used. Tin cans are still used for the preservation of fruits, vegetables, soups and sauces. Though they are called tin cans they are actually steel with a very thin coating of tin. Tin is very rare and there are few tin mines. It can be rolled very thinly. A pound of tin can be rolled thinly enough to cover 130 square feet. Tin, however, is used as the thin coating because it is not affected by the acidity of the foods in the can. Some tin cans available today have ring tabs on top permitting a person to open the can without the use of a can opener.

The aluminum can was first used by the Coors Brewing Company in 1959. Coors, at the time, offered one cent for any cans returned to them so they could be recycled. Aluminum cans are extremely recyclable. 70 percent of its material can be recycled many times. The aluminum can was capable of cooling the beer much faster than the tin can. Additionally, the lighter weight had shipping advantages. In 1962, the Aluminum Company of America (Alcoa) produced aluminum cans for the Pittsburgh Brewing Company. It is now used for all beer, soft drinks and sport drinks.

12. Tupperware

This revolutionary idea in food storage was the invention of Earl Tupper in 1942. His assortment of food storage containers have a unique seal requiring a "burping" action to eliminate the air inside the container and thereby prolonging the freshness of its contents. Mr. Tupper started selling his products in 1948. Sales were accomplished by "Tupperware parties" starting in 1949. Those parties were mainly hosted by women who wanted the self-esteem and income of having their own business. Tupperware Brands is still going strong in almost 100 countries. Its revenue was 2.26 billion dollars in 2017.

13. Twist ties

These small pieces of wire embedded in a plastic or paper covering were the brainchild of George Hinson in 1923. Mr. Hinson's had only a paper covering. Plastics weren't available at that time. The idea was put to use by Charles Burford when he started tying bread sacks with them. It kept the bread fresh much longer. Now they are used to tie storage and trash bags. Many of the manufacturers of trash bags include twist ties with the bags. Some people have a small bag of twist ties in a drawer waiting for their 'call to duty'. Do you?

Electronic & communication items

14. Cassette tape

The cassette tape was invented by the engineers of the Phillips Company of Belgium in 1962. They featured it in the Berlin Air Show in August of 1963. It was introduced into the United States in November of 1963, just in time for the frenzied Christmas shopping.

15. Cell phone

No.1 on many peoples' list of inventions that weigh less than 16 ounces. That is why this book is in alphabetical order. What would you rank as No. 2, No. 3 etc. all the way through 100? Many believe the cell phone is the most important invention in the history of the world, more important than fire or the wheel which were No. 1 & No. 2. The first camera for a cellular phone was the Samsung SCH-V200 available in South Korea in June of 2000. It had to be hooked up to a computer to get the pictures. In November of 2000 Sharp released a camera in Japan that allowed you to send the pictures electronically without being hooked up. It was November 2002 (isn't it weird that all these releases are just before the Christmas shopping frenzy) when the U.S. could get the Sanyo SCP-5300 on Sprint. It cost $400. By the end of 2003 over 80 million camera phones had been sold worldwide.

Using a cell phone is a temporary thing. You're only going to be able to use it while the battery has some life in it. Then you must re-charge it using the 'battery charger'. Should the battery charger be one of the hundred on this list? The cell phone has a lifespan of only several hours without it.

16. Compact disc (CD)

The CD was invented by James Russell in 1968. Mr. Russell was a physicist. He was born in Bremerton, Washington in 1931. He was employed by Phillips and Sony. The first CD's sold commercially was in 1980. By 1982 it had replaced the cassette tape in popularity.

17. Digital Video Disc (DVD)

The engineers of Sony Corporation and Phillips Electronics NV started developing the DVD, also known as a Digital Versatile Disc for its ability to play data, from their knowledge of the compact disc. They succeeded in 1995 and the DVD was born. There was another format which was developed by Toshiba Corporation and Time Warner Inc. The two competing groups agreed on a common format and the DVD was ready to entertain the world. The first DVD players were sold in Japan in 1996.

18. Garage door operator

Oh, the many times we've been able to pull the car into the garage and avoid the rain or snow that is falling. Even on nice days it gives us a sense of security to be able to pull into the garage and not worry about what or who may be lurking outside. Close the door quickly before they can follow you. You're not being paranoid. You're only being cautious.

The electric garage door operator was invented by C. G. Johnson of Hartford City, Indiana in 1926. Initially it was operated by pressing a button affixed to the wall. Now it is activated by a battery operated hand-held electronic device.

Mr. Johnson's invention spawned the birth of the Overhead Door Company. It currently has its general offices in Dallas, Texas. It was purchased in 1996 by Sanwa Holdings Corporation of Tokyo.

19. Solar cell

Leonardo da Vinci was interested in turning the power of the sun into energy but it was not until 1883 that Charles Fritts invented the first solar battery. He used selenium with a very thin coating of gold. It only converted about one percent of the sun's energy into electricity. In 1941 Russell Ohl invented the silicon solar cell. Bell Laboratories had funded research in solar cells and in 1954 three researchers, Gerald Pearson, Calvin Fuller and Daryl Chapin invented a solar cell capable of capturing six percent of the sun's energy. They had placed an array of silicon strips in sunlight. They captured the free electrons and turned them into electricity. Bell used their invention to create and produce a solar battery. The first public demonstration of its use was on a telephone carrier system at Americus, Georgia on October 4, 1955. Solar cells were used on the Vanguard 1 satellite in 1958. The power necessary for the daily functions and experiments of the International Space Station (ISS) is provided by solar cells in an array of solar panels. The space station spends 35 minutes of every 90 minute revolution in darkness. The 55 minutes spent in sunlight collect the light and convert it into electricity in each of its 262,400 solar cells. Each of them weighs less than 16 ounces but together they occupy eight solar arrays. Each array is 112 feet long by 39 feet wide. The arrays total about 27,000 square feet in area.

20. Spark plug

The first spark plug, a device to provide a spark to ignite a fuel/air mixture, was probably invented by Edmond Berger, an immigrant from Togo, in 1839. It was an invention without a purpose at the time because the sparkplug was needed to provide ignition in an internal combustion engine which hadn't been developed at the time. A German inventor, Robert Bosch, invented the first functioning spark plug in 1901. He was issued a patent in 1902. Early forms of the spark plug were made of porcelain that could not withstand the extreme heat generated in the engines. In 1915, the

Frenchtown Porcelain Company developed a 775 degree heat porcelain which was capable of withstanding the heat. Diesel engines do not require spark plugs as the stroke of the engine provides enough heat for ignition.. Electric cars do not require spark plugs as there is no fuel to ignite.

21. Transistors

This tiny device is all around you. There are billions in your smart phone and more than that in your laptop or desktop computer. None of the electronics we know today would have been possible without William Shockley, Walter Brattain and John Bardeen who invented the Transistor in 1947.

Transistors are basically miniature switches answering a million yes or no questions and turning them off and/or on at the speed of light.

That makes one wonder how the speed of light was determined. Galileo, way back in 1638, conducted an experiment trying to find the answer. He had an assistant with a lantern stand on top of a hill which was a measured distance from the top of the hill he stood with his lantern. At precisely the same moment, they removed the cover of their lanterns. Galileo was going to clock the intervening time. Of course there was none. 38 years later, in 1676, Ole Roemer experimented with the interval of time it took IO, a moon of Jupiter, to travel the orbit of the Earth. His experiment determined the speed of light to be 227,000,000 meters per second. That is approximately 142,000 miles per second. In 1849, Hippolyte Fizau, a French physicist, used a toothed wheel and rotating mirrors to establish the speed. His calculations resulted in a speed of 313,000,000 meters/second. Leon Foucault, another French physicist and sometime colleague of Fizau, using basically the same method, resulted in a speed of 298,000,000 meters/second. Experiments conducted by Marie Alfred Cornu and Albert A. Michelson in 1926 established the speed at 299,760,000 meters/ second. Since then it's been refined to 299,722,458 meters/second. Which is 186,282 miles per second. As far as is known, no one has disputed that and no one is conducting further experiments.

22. T.V. remote

The No. 1 invention of couch potatoes everywhere. This boon to the convenience of man has totally eliminated the exercise program of many individuals, i.e. getting up and changing the channel manually.

As far back as 1893, Nikola Tesla, a Croatian Engineer and physicist, explained a remote control. Tesla emigrated to the U.S. in 1884 to work for the Edison Electric Company, (yes, that's Thomas Edison). They discontinued their association amid heated arguments of which was better, direct current supplying electricity (Edison's view) or alternating current (Tesla's view). Tesla's alternating current won. That is what we use today. Tesla died in 1943. He was the holder of 300 patents. He is a member of the IHOF. The amount of force exerted in a magnetic resonance imager (an M.R.I.} is a tesla, named to honor him. Since Tesla's early demonstration of remote control we have come far. Zenith Radio Corporation created the first TV remote in 1950. It was not wireless but had a cable from the TV set that would extend to the chair or sofa of the viewer. It was somewhat hazardous as people tripped over the cable. Mr. Eugene Polley, a Zenith engineer, created a wireless remote in 1955. It had four photocells that controlled the functions of the remote, channel selection and sound volume. The photocells were affected by sunlight filtering into the room during the daylight hours. Another Zenith engineer, Robert Adler, created a remote using ultrasound. It had a receiver inside the TV that had six vacuum tubes to receive the commands of the remote. It costs 30% more to buy a TV with the remote than one without. The invention and subsequent popularity of the transistor allowed the replacement of the vacuum tubes and the consequent savings. Where would we be today without the transistor?

Perhaps the 'previous channel and mute buttons' should be separate items on this list but they are integral to the remote itself. So, they're not.

23. Vacuum tube

The vacuum tube was present in our homes, automobiles, trucks, offices and factories throughout the first half of the twentieth century. It was the thing that permitted us to know the news and the weather forecast as well as enjoy the sounds of the big bands. The vacuum tubes were hidden inside the table top, dashboard and console of our radios and televisions. They are what made those radios and televisions work. The first practical vacuum tube was invented by John Ambrose Montgomery in 1904. Vacuum tubes were used in all radios and televisions until the transistor was invented in 1947. The vacuum tubes quickly became obsolete because of the transistor. The only vacuum tubes being produced now are specialty tubes. There is a new business today based on salvaging vacuum tubes and selling the rare items for much more than the original cost. If you're interested in making that old radio or TV operational, find a source, grab your wallet or purse and go out the door. Good luck, you'll need it.

Health & beauty items

24. Cotton swabs

Mr. Leo Gerstenzang had an inspiration in 1921 when he saw his wife trying to get some cotton to adhere to a toothpick to clean some crevices. He applied cotton to both ends of a rolled paper stick and the cotton swab was born. He called the product Baby Gays until 1923 when he changed the name to Q-tips. Gerstenzang was born in Warsaw, Poland in 1892. He moved to the United States in 1912 and became a U.S. citizen in 1919. He founded the Leo Gerstenzang

Infant Novelty Co. to manufacture the product. The swabs were initially manufactured with a wooden stick. Plastic sticks replaced them until recently when the company went to a rolled paper stick. The plastic sticks were being washed into the seas and oceans and becoming a hazard to marine life. The company was acquired by Cheseborough-Ponds in1962 and then by Unilever in 1987. Q-tips has annual sales of $200 million dollars. The science quad at Brandeis University in the Boston suburb of Waltham, Massachusetts is named in honor of Mr. Gerstenzang.

25. Soap

The first recorded use of a soap-like substance goes way, way back to the Babylonians in 2800 B.C. They used animal fat and ashes to make it. Since animal fat and ashes cannot be considered some of the cleanest things in the world, you may wonder why the Babylonians thought the combination of the two would make a cleansing agent. Is it 'two wrongs make a white? Today's soaps are very particular about their ingredients. They will not use the fat from just any animal. There is a fat list of acceptable fats. If you're not on the list, no soap.

26. Tissues

These soft, thin pieces of paper, were introduced to the public as Kleenex® by Kimberly Clark Corporation in 1924. There are many other brands available now. The tissues have a unique packaging system. They are folded in such a way that a new tissue pops up from the box as you withdraw one. The tissues were to be primarily used to remove cold cream and make-up. Since then, people have used them from top to bottom to wipe things that need wiping. Details of wipeable things are not necessary, are they?

4

Medical items

27. Adhesive bandages

It happens to everyone. You are intent on fixing something or repairing something and in your haste you scrape a knuckle or cut your finger or some other minor mishaps that bleeds. It is not serious enough to go to the ER or require stitches. It is a troubling situation where you would have to find a piece of cloth and adhesive tape to apply to the wound. That problem was eliminated in 1920 when Earle Dickson of the Johnson and Johnson Company invented the Band-aid®.

This little piece of tape with a piece of gauze attached was an instant hit. It was especially appreciated by mothers who had to bandage their children's mishaps they received while playing nicely as they were told to do.

28. Artificial heart

The Smithsonian Institution has an artificial heart on display that is the invention of Domingo Liotta was implanted into 47 year old Mr. Haskell Karp on April 4, 1969 by Doctor Denton Cooley. Mr. Karp survived three days until a human heart was found and implanted in him. Unfortunately, Mr. Karp lived for only two days after it was implanted. Paul Winchell, a man best known as an actor, ventriloquist and comedian, was granted patent #3097366 for an artificial heart. He had advice from Dr. Henry Heimlich, renowned for the Heimlich Maneuver used to prevent persons from choking, in designing it. Mr. Winchell had an ambition to be a doctor and had studied medicine at Columbia University. He was the holder of 30 patents many of which were for medical devices. Controversy developed about the subsequent invention of an artificial heart by Dr. Robert Jarvik. Dr.

Heimlich believed the heart copied Winchell's design and a patent should not have been issued. However, it was. The Jarvik-7 heart was implanted in Dr. Barney Clark, a dentist, on December 2, 1982 by Dr. William DeVries. Dr. Clark lived four months after the implant. He had been expected to die within days without it. By 1985 six more patients received the Jarvik-7. One died within ten days from bleeding. The others survived from 7.5 months to 11 years. There have been more than 350 implants of the Jarvik-7 to date.

29. Dentures

Before the invention of toothpaste, people were lackadaisical about dental care. It resulted in severe dental problems including loose, rotten teeth. Those rotten teeth caused all sort of problems to the individual. I am not going to mention the foul breath that others had to endure. (I did mention it, didn't I? My bad.). Those rotten teeth would have to be removed from that suffering person's mouth, not to mention the suffering of the recipients of the foul breath. It was a very painful experience to have teeth removed since it was before the advent of anesthetics. Then, after the teeth were removed, the person could not eat any of those chewy foods they loved such as beef jerky and corn on the cob. It is very difficult to chew chewy foods if you don't have teeth in which to chew them. There were attempts for hundreds, if not thousands, of years to construct 'false teeth' that are serviceable and comfortable. Those teeth were made of ivory and various precious metals. They were much too costly for most people, so, consequently, those people went toothless. Then, much cheaper porcelain teeth were invented by Alex Duchateau in 1770. By that time George Washington already had dentures. If he'd waited for the porcelain ones he would have saved a lot of money. However, if he had waited there would have been all those years without any beef jerky, corn on the cob or whatever was his chewy food preference. Washington was a wealthy man. He didn't have to wait for cheaper dentures. His dentures were made of ivory. They were not made of wood as you may have heard.

30. Eye glasses

Man has always wanted to have the eyes of an eagle or a hawk.so he can see more clearly. The eagles and the hawks do not willingly give up their eyes. They are not even interested in a trade such as 'you give me yours and I'll give you mine and I'll throw in two mice and a rabbit to sweeten the deal'. Realizing the impossibility of such a trade, man embarked on other ways to improve his eyesight. He tried squinting, but it did not result in the increase in sight he wanted. Sometime along about the 6th CBE the Chinese used polished jewels to peer through and improve their sight. This was not an ideal solution as the majority of the Chinese could not afford polished jewels. The Emperor Nero would hold a polished emerald in front of his eyes to reduce the glare from the gladiators swords as they killed each other. Improvement in the ability to see for many people was delayed until sometime between 1268 and 1300 when the first corrective lenses were made. This was shortly after Roger Bacon invented the convex lens in 1260 or so. Those first corrective lenses were convex lenses which helped the farsighted people see. The nearsighted had to wait until the early 16th century when concave lenses were made. Those early lenses were separated by a wire that was spread apart and then clamped over the bridge of the nose. These *pince nez* glasses were made until 1730 when Edward Scarlett, a London optician, fashioned two rods onto the lenses so the rods would rest on the top of a person's ears. James Ayscough, an eyeglass designer and maker of scientific instruments, refined the design of eyeglasses by adding hinges so the rods could be folded. That occurred about 1752. The only major change since then was in 1784 when Benjamin Franklin invented bifocals.

31. Hearing aids

The common use of hearing aids today does not indicate the Herculean struggle that has taken place over time by the husbands and wives of days gone by. Innumerable times, if we'd listened closely we'd have heard; "I told you the other day." "No you didn't, this is the first I've heard of it." "Regardless, you have to be ready by seven because we have to leave then if we're going to be on time" "If you had told me earlier, I would be ready." "I did tell you. You can't hear. You need hearing aids." Does that sound familiar? Have you heard it? If not, you may need hearing aids. It happens all the time. Luckily, the hearing aids available today are much more effective than the piece of hollow cow horn people used as an ear trumpet in the centuries before Miller Hutchison invented the first electric hearing aid in 1898. It was called the Akuophone. Mr. Hutchison invention of the hearing aid was helped immensely by Alexander Graham Bell's invention of the telephone in 1876. Mr. Bell had been able to identify the technology needed to control loudness, frequency and distortion which are required in a hearing aid. Then, in 1911, Louis Weber made another hearing aid called the Esha Phonophor. Mr. Hutchison's and Mr. Weber's hearing aids were not portable. They were table-top devices with wires leading to speakers to be inserted in the ears. In the late 1800's Thomas Edison invented a carbon transmitter to assist in hearing. The first commercially available hearing aids were sold in 1913. They contained vacuum tubes and were not portable. The modern hearing aids contain transistors, as do so many of today's products, enabling the hearing aid to be inserted in the ear. World-wide there are at least eight hearing aid manufacturers.

32. Hypodermic needle

The development of the hypodermic needle by Dr. Alexander Wood and Charles Pravaz in 1853 has been a lifesaver. That term is not being used frivolously but seriously. In the last one and three-quarters centuries There are individuals who must periodically inject themselves with lifesaving medications. We can all be thankful for the various "shots" we have available or we've received to prevent diseases or conditions that, in the 18th century and before, would have been debilitating or fatal. Hypodermic needles have gotten a bad rap from being used to inject dangerous, illegal substances. That is not the fault of the needle. The word hypodermic is derived from the Greek, hypo meaning under and dermic meaning skin. The song would not have been nearly as popular if it had been titled 'I've got you hypo my dermic'.

33. Pacemaker

This is most likely No. 1, the most important invention, of the millions of people who have a pacemaker placed inside them to regulate their heartbeat. The invention of the pacemaker was a work of many individuals. John Hoops, a Canadian engineer, had developed a pacemaker in 1950. It was not implantable. A patent #3,057,356 was issued October 9, 1962 to Dr. Wilson Greatbatch for an implantable pacemaker. He had been collaborating since the mid-fifties with Drs. William Chardack and Andrew Gage for the development of a pacemaker for the heart. They implanted one in a dog in 1958. They refined the design and in 1960 implanted a pacemaker in a 77 year old man. He lived for an additional 10 months. They implanted nine others that year. Some of those patients lived for twenty years. The earliest pacemakers were capable of regulating cardiac rhythm of the ventricle, the bottom chamber of the heart. With the advent of the lithium battery in 1969 pacemakers became more sophisticated and could regulate both the lower and the upper, atrium, chamber. The present sophistications signal the patient when the battery is getting low and needs replacing.

34. Thermometer

The mercury thermometer we use today was invented by Daniel Fahrenheit in 1714. Yes, it's his name, Fahrenheit, we use to measure degrees of heat. Some people, never content with what others have done, are compelled to make changes. Anders Celsius was one of those. He introduced a new scale for measuring heat called the centigrade scale. It is now referred to as the Celsius scale. He would have been so happy. The Celsius scale has the freezing point of water at zero degrees and the boiling point at one hundred degrees. The Fahrenheit scale has the freezing point of water at thirty-two degrees and the boiling point at two hundred twelve degrees. There are medical thermometers for measuring body temperature. Ninety- six point eight degrees is normal. Any bodily temperature varying six degrees from normal is cause for concern. Medical thermometers cover both ends, not referring to Fahrenheit or Celsius, but to oral and anal, depending on where you stick them. Please have them well marked, heads or tails, to differentiate their purpose.

Miscellaneous items

35. Aerosol can

Two employees of the United States Department of Agriculture, Lyle Goodhue and W. N. Sullivan created a small can pressurized by liquified gas in 1943. They created it to dispense mosquito killing insecticide to protect the American soldiers fighting in the jungle campaigns of the Second World War. Mr. Goodhue was a prolific inventor. He was the holder of 105 U. S. patents and 25 foreign ones. He died in 1981. Mr. Goodhue and Mr. Sullivan's aerosol can was not the first. Mr. Erik

Rotheim of Oslo, Norway was granted a patent for a spray can in 1927. A U. S. patent was issued in 1931. Mr. Rotheim sold his rights to the patent. Mr. Robert Alplanalp, an American engineer, was issued a patent on March 17. 1953 for an aerosol valve. Mr. Alplanalp founded the Precision Valve Corporation and began manufacturing the valve. The creation of the aerosol can spawned a new industry manufacturing a variety of products in aerosol cans. One of the first was paint in aerosol cans. Initially the only color was aluminum. There are now a multitude of colors available. Aerosol cans now dispense cleaners, insecticides, cooking spray, dessert topping, cheese and hair spray. Helene Curtis has SprayNet available for those who want to keep their hair nicely coiffed while riding in a convertible.

36. Batteries

They give us light. They give us joy. They give us comfort. They give us help. They give us as much as they've got for as long as they can. Then, most times they are discarded if we have given enough thought to get replacements. Alessandro Volta invented the first modern battery around 1800. Volta was an Italian physicist, chemist and electricity pioneer. To honor him, a unit of electricity is called a volt. Benjamin Franklin coined the term "battery" in 1748 describing an array of glass plates. In the 1780's Luigi Galvani did research allowing Alessandro Volta to invent his Voltaic Pile in 1800. It produced electrical current. It was a "wet cell battery".

John F. Daniel, an Englishman, invented the Daniel Cell in 1836. It produced a "dry cell battery" using a zinc sulfate and a copper sulfate electrolyte. It produced about 1.1 volts. In 1866 Georges Leclanche used ammonium chloride paste for his moist electrolyte thereby creating the first "dry cell battery".

Carl Gassner invented a zinc-carbon dry cell battery in 1881. It was the first to be commercially successful.

Lew Urry, an employee of the Eveready Battery Company, invented the alkaline battery in 1949. They last five to eight times longer than the zinc carbon ones.

Some automobiles now use a dry cell battery. They do not emit gasses and there is no lead-acid fluid to spill. It gets its current from a moist paste electrolyte.

The standard "D" cell battery used in flashlights weighs 3.3 ounces. The flashlight with 2 "D batteries weighs between 11 and 12 ounces.

William Robert Grove produced the first fuel cell in 1839. Improvements have continued to be made over the years including the rechargeable battery of Gaston Plante of France in 1859.

37. Candles

Candles were the prevalent source of night-time light in the time of the ancient Mesopotamians or some-such. That remained the case until the end of the nineteenth century. It is believed that human habitation began in the Mesopotamia area as early as 14,000 BCE. Did they have some form of candle-like torch? We know candle-like torches have been in existence as far back as 3000 BCE Some type of wicked candle has been used by most cultures. The Egyptians used rolled papyrus as the wick. The Romans had wicked candles they used for lighting and religious ceremonies. The Chinese used rolled rice paper for the wick. The Japanese candle wax came from tree nuts and in India the wax came from the fruit of the cinnamon tree. So cinnamon smelling candles are not a new innovation. The majority of candle wax was the fat of animals rendered into tallow. Beeswax was also used but it was very expensive and therefore unavailable to most people. Beeswax candles burned with a sweet smell and without the smoke which emanated from the tallow wax candles of the common man. There was a candle-making guild starting in the 13th century. The guild members, they are known as chandlers, would visit the homes of citizens and make candles from the animal fat the wife had saved for that purpose. The late 18th century saw the use of whale fat rendered into candle wax. It produced a sweet smelling, less smoky candle that was able to withstand summer heat without collapsing. A French chemist, Michel Eugene Chevreul, discovered a way to extract stearic acid from animal fat. This permitted the development of stearin wax. Stearin wax is hard and burns cleanly. M. Chevreul's discovery occurred in the 1820's. Stearin wax candles are still available in Europe. A man named Joseph Morgan invented a machine in 1834 that could eject molded candles as soon as they solidified. This was a major improvement in candle-making and increased the production of candles significantly. That allowing them to become cheaper and available to more people. The advent of paraffin for use as candle wax began in the 1850's. Chemists discovered how to separate the paraffin from petroleum and refine it. Paraffin wax is odorless, burns cleanly and is cheaper to produce. Its only drawback is its low melting point. Chemists overcame that by adding stearic acid to the paraffin. The use of candles for interior lighting decreased significantly at the end of the 19th and the beginning of the 20th centuries. The use of gaslight in the 19th and the availability of electric power in the 20th made the use of candlelight unrealistic. Today candles are used mainly as decorative items, mood-setters and gifts.

There is a National Candle Association

529 14th St NW

Washington, DC 20045

38. Cellophane

Cellophane was the first plastic film that was transparent enabling you to see its contents. It was invented in 1900 by a man named Jacques E. Brandenberger. He was born in Zurich, Switzerland in 1872. He was at a restaurant and someone spilled wine onto the tablecloth ruining it. He thought there must be a way to make a cloth that is impervious to such accidents. A cloth that would shed the liquid instead of allowing it to soak in. He started experimenting in an effort to find such a cloth. He started by spraying a viscose waterproofing onto a fabric but the fabric became too stiff to achieve the result he wanted. He started over use cellulose fibers from wood. He combined them with carbon disulfide. After extruding it through a narrow slit and with an acid bath it becomes a film. Cellophane. That is name Mr. Brandenberger called it. He combined the words cellulose and diaphane, a French word meaning transparent. Brandenberger also, in 1912, designed the machinery necessary to produce it. Production of cellophane started in 1920. Brandenberger sold the U. S. production rights to DuPont Company in 1923. Cellophane at that time was not moisture-proof. Water vapor could seep in. The problem was solved in 1927 by William Hale Charch, a DuPont employee. That improvement made it suitable for food packaging and opened a large new market for the product.

39. Cigarette lighter

The most ubiquitous cigarette lighter is manufactured by the Zippo® Manufacturing Company of Bradford, Pennsylvania. They sold their five hundred millionth unit in 2012 and are still going strong. Their brushed chrome model is the one carried by millions of smokers around the world. The Zippo® lighter was the invention of George Blaisdell in 1932. He started manufacturing them in 1933. There were other lighters on the market but most were heavier, more cumbersome and required both hands to operate. Blaisdell's could be operated with one hand which meant you did not have to set down your beer to light a cigarette. Blaisdell's Zippo® was not as heavy (a lighter lighter?) and the flip-open case restricted the wind from blowing out the flame. The Ronson lighter was the most popular of cigarette lighters before the Zippo. They were manufactured by the Art Metal Works of Newark, New Jersey. The company was founded in 1897 by Louis V. Aronson. Mr. Aronson applied for a patent for a lighter in 1913. The company introduced the Banjo design lighter in 1926. It had a lever you would push to activate it.

When you released the lever the flame would be extinguished. Ronson introduced the Mastercase lighter in 1933. It sold for $7.95. That is equivalent to about $150.00 today. The art-deco style, the high cost and the weight of Ronson lighters allowed Zippo to become No. 1.

Zippo remained No. 1 until 1973. That was the year the Bic lighter was introduced. The Bic lighter was invented by Baron Marcel Bich (pronounced Bic) of Clichy, France. Baron Bich owned a factory in which he manufactured very successful ball-point pens. He retooled and started to manufacture lighters as well as pens. Bic sold 1.6 billion lighters in 2016. Bic lighters are a miniature butane torch. Though close in operation and construction they normally serve two different purposes. The butane torch is used to light BBQ grills and fireplaces. It is also larger than the cigarette lighter. Dr, Walter Snelling discovered butane in 1912. Butane torches are also used in craft projects, glass making and caramelizing desserts.

It is very easy to operate the Bic lighter. You press the top lever, a spark ignites the flame, the flame is extinguished when you release the lever. As a bonus, even though all of them are called a cigarette lighter, they are equally capable of lighting cigars. Whoopee.

40. Compass

This item is not referring to the V- shaped device used to draw circles, even though that device is a great invention, but the device with a suspended needle that points to magnetic North. The fundamental design of a compass was developed in China during the Qin dynasty (221 – 206 BCE). The Han dynasty (20 BCE – 20 CE) used a lodestone which has magnetic properties as a compass. It was used for navigation by sea-going traders about the 10th century. By the Renaissance Period (which was 1400 to 1600 or 1300 to 1700. Take your pick) compasses were using a dry method where the needle swung about on a fixed axis. Columbus would have had a compass on his journeys to the new world. Without one he may have sailed in circles for years and years never finding land. Where would we be then? We would be somewhere but we may not be 'here'. We wouldn't have been able to find 'here'. The compass may not inform you of where you are, but it will let you know which direction you traveled to get there.

41. Credit cards

Before the second half of the twentieth century, when you wanted to buy something, you had to have the money to pay for it. Not anymore. Diners Club changed all that. It was the first credit card company. It was founded in 1950 by Frank X. McNamara, Ralph Schneider, Matty Simmons and Alfred S. Bloomingdale. Diners Club permitted you to visit restaurants and charge your meal to your Diners Club card. The idea expanded over the next decade so it includes all merchandise and service organizations. You present the little plastic card, the credit card, and not have to pay for it at that time. The financial institution that gave you the little plastic credit card will pay for it temporarily. They will lend you the money to buy the item and bill you for it within a month. They'll give you two or three weeks to send the money to them to pay for the item. If money has gotten tight for you at that time, they'll give you more time to pay the bill. They will be most happy to give you more time. They'll charge you interest on the unpaid balance of up to eighteen percent. The proliferation of credit cards since the first one, the Diners Club card, in 1950 is overwhelming. It seems every major business and all banks have their own credit card. We receive, in the mail and on television, constant invitations to accept one of their cards hoping we will use it to buy something we can't afford and pay the interest accumulating on the unpaid balance every month. Now we have the debit card. It was started by the Bank of Delaware in 1966. The use of debit cards increased significantly in the 80s and '90s. The financial institution normally charges a user fee of $1.00 to $3.00 per month for a debit card. In addition, there is a swipe fee of forty to fifty cents for each transaction. The convenience of having a credit card is worth it. Isn't it?

42. Glass

Glass was first made about 3500 BCE. It is primarily silica sand heated until it melts and becomes liquid. That requires an extreme temperature of about 3600 degrees

Fahrenheit (that's fifty times hotter than your comfort zone of 72 degrees). Glass is very heavy. The thinnest standard glass thickness is 3/32 inch (2.4mm). It weighs 19.7 ounces per square foot. That would make it ineligible for inclusion in this list. However, as stated in "Things you need to know", article 3, 16 oz. or less in their basic configuration and article 6, man-made or manufactured item. A common 8" x 12" window pane weighs 13.1 ounces.

Glass is used to make a wide variety of things that weigh less than 16 ounces. Things for the betterment or delight of mankind that require much less than a square foot of it. There are bottles, vases, dishes and bowls. One of the most useful objects is the water glass. We need to be thankful for the water glass. Most people's hands aren't large enough to scoop up enough water to quench their thirst. They must bend over time after time to get enough water. The water glass solves this serious problem for most people. Fill it and drink until you've had enough and if not, fill it again. It is called a 'water glass' but don't let it dissuade you from filling it with a different beverage of your choice. The glass will accept any liquid you want.

There are many other things that require glass. The next item on this list, the light bulb, requires glass to enclose the filament. Also, without glass we would be unable to see ourselves as others see us. There would be no mirrors. The first person to see what they looked like was most likely the reflection seen in a pool of water. Throughout time mankind has made efforts to see what he looks like. Some early examples of this are the mirrors, made of black obsidian glass, found in Turkish ruins dating back to 6000 b.c. The Egyptians, Mesopotamians and the Chinese used polished copper to view their reflection 2000 years ago. The Aztecs used polished stones. Mirrors of metal backed glass were made in Lebanon in the first century AD. Mirrors have always been associated with various superstitions, most of them being the belief that the mirror is associated with a person's soul. Breaking a mirror means seven years bad luck refers to the concept of the soul taking seven years to regenerate. The modern mirror was the invention of Justus von Liebig, a German chemist. In 1835 Mr. von Liebig put a thin layer of metallic silver to the back of a pane of glass. The process allowed manufacturers to produce mirrors at a reasonable price. Prior to then, mirrors were very expensive and only the wealthy could afford them.

43. Light bulbs

Thomas Edison invented the incandescent bulb in 1879. Edison's incandescent bulb was the first commercially viable incandescent bulb. There were other light bulbs but none capable of sustaining the light long enough to be commercially accepted. Edison started producing them in his General Electric Company. Those first light bulbs used a tungsten filament. That's the part that burns giving off light. The light they produced used only one-third of the electric current it received. Subsequent development of the fluorescent bulb and the compact fluorescent bulb (CFL) uses ninety percent of the electric supplied to them. The past thirty years has seen the development of the LED (Item No. 21) bulb. The LED bulb uses one-fifth the energy of the incandescent bulb to provide the same amount of light. The electric companies are offering budget packages of LED bulbs to get us to use them. Should we applaud the electric companies for pushing us to use LED's? They're the only company coming to mind that want us to use *less* of their product.

44. Magnets

The legend has it that a man named Magnus, a shepherd, sat on a rock while attending his sheep. His hob-nail boots stuck to the rock when he tried to stand. The rock was of the ones called 'magnetite'. That, supposedly, was man-kinds first experience with magnetism. Magnets are now produced commercially for many different purposes from tiny rings and discs to an assortment of magnets holding your photos and notes on the refrigerator. The use of magnets for that purpose relieves your mind from the possibility that the wind blew your sticky note off the fridge. There are huge magnets in a Magnetic Resonating Imager, a life saver in many instances. The simplest current into a coil of wire wrapped around a piece of iron such as a nail.

45. Magnifying glass

The magnifying glass was invented centuries ago by Roger Bacon, the renowned researcher in the laws of refraction and reflection. He invented the magnifying glass in the year 1260 or so. He did not invent the magnifying glass we know today as a lens in a frame with a handle to hold the frame. He invented the convex lens. His discovery has led to a multitude of items for the benefit of mankind throughout the years. The basic premise of the magnifying glass is the use of a curved piece of glass to have objects appear closer and therefore more distinct. Telescopes, microscopes, binoculars, and eyeglasses are versions of the magnifying glass.

46. Matches

The invention of matches relieved man from the burden of carrying a flint and a stone to start a fire. It is especially difficult to light a candle which were the primary source of night-time lighting until the 19th century, using a flint. Monsieur Jean Chancel invented a match in 1805 that had to be dipped in sulfuric acid to ignite. It was not extremely popular. Charles Sauria developed a match in 1830 that was apt to drop its burning end onto your floor or onto you. Needless to say, it too was not overwhelmingly popular and was subsequently outlawed. Gustav Eric Pasch and John Edvard Lundstrom started selling a match in 1858 that neither dropped its burning end nor had to be dipped in acid. Theirs was much more popular and safer. Matches come in several sizes and two materials. There are wooden ones and paper ones. Joshua Posey invented paper book matches in 1892. All the matches have one end covered with a sulfur and red phosphorous mixture that will burst into flame when struck on an abrasive surface, unless it's gotten wet. Then, reach for your flint and stone.

47. Needles

These are some of the lightest items on the list but one of the most diverse in purpose. The tissue is also lightweight but not nearly as diverse. The date of needles first being used is lost somewhere in the distant past. However, Jesus Christ refers to the eye of a needle to point out the difficulty a rich man has in going to heaven. There are needles for sewing cloth by hand or machine. The things we wear daily, the clothes and shoes, have been assembled using needles. Buttons would be just an ornamental disc without a needle and thread to attach them. There are crocheting needles and knitting needles.* There are surgical needles and phonograph needles. There are large needles used to sew canvas and leather. There is another kind of needle that is of major importance to the health and well- being of everyone. It is important enough to have its own listing. It is the hypodermic needle which is an entry in Medical items.

* The impetus for the invention of knitting and crocheting needles was the overwhelming desire of grandmothers to make something special for the newest member of the family. Through the years these wonderful, proud matriarchs have provided so much warmth to the little tykes. There are knitted blankets, little knitted hoodies that tie under the baby's chubby chin, and little mittens with a cord tying the left and the right one together so you can lose both at the same time. The grandfather is also included in this project. He has to assure the grandmother she will not lose visiting rights to the new-born if she doesn't finish the knitting in time. Stick to your knitting, grandma. You'll get it finished.

48. Photographs

This does not refer to cameras. This is pictures. We have come a long way in the two hundred years photographs have been in existence. Is there a person in the civilized world who hasn't laughed or cried at photos of people or events? Today, more photos are taken with cell phones than with cameras.

Cell phones allow us to see the pictures immediately. You have the option of accepting them or deleting them. You may delete them if something drastic happens such as your mouth is open or your hair is a mess.

However, none of this would have happened without the invention of the camera. The camera was not invented by a single person. There were many innovative individuals who through countless experimentation developed the camera. One of the primary innovators was Joseph Nicephore Niepce of France around 1816. He used a silver chloride covered paper to capture an image. There are no details of what the image was or how long it lasted before fading into obscurity. That was a major problem. How to retain the image for a long period of time. Mr. Niepce had a collaborator named Louis Daguerre. M. Daguerre continued with their experiments in longevity after Mr. Niecpe's death in 1833. Mr. Daguerre was successful and introduced his Daguerretype photos to the world in 1839. The original cameras were big, boxy things weighing much more than 16 ounces. Still, it is interesting to know some of the evolution of those big, boxy things until the present when cameras are only one of the functions of the cell phone. Cameras became immensely popular after George Eastman developed the Kodak camera in 1888. It used a roll of film and not the plates necessary for the big boxy cameras. Though quite large and boxy itself, it was much less than other available cameras. Kodak became the leading manufacturer of cameras. The lead increased dramatically when Kodak introduced their Brownie model in 1927. The Brownie made it possible for everyone to afford a camera and become a photographer. Mr. Eastman became tremendously wealthy selling film for his cameras. The photos taken at the start of photography were all black and white photos. James Clerk Maxwell, a Scottish physicist and mathematician, is credited with being the inventor of color photography by his use of red, blue and yellow filters in 1861. That initial success in producing color photography whotography.as improved upon over the succeeding years. Gabriel Lippman won the Nobel Prize in physics in 1908 for his method of producing color photos. It was followed by the work of Valenta in Vienna and Lumiere in Lyon. It was 1935 before Kodak sold their first color film. It was called Kodachrome and included the cost of developing it. However, and there is always a however, it didn't include the cost of prints. Kodak stopped developing film in 1988. By 2008 the demand for Kodachrome film had reduced precipitously. That year they produced only one mile long sheet of the film. It was cut into 20,000 rolls. The first all-color full-length movie was The World, the Flesh and the Devil in 1914. The first technicolor movie was The Gulf Between in 1917. Snow White and the Seven Dwarfs was the first full-length animated movie in color. It was released in 1937.

49. Plastic

You are surrounded by it. Look around, If you are anywhere in the civilized world you are surrounded by products made of some kind of plastic in one of its thousand variations. Though there are thousands of variations, plastic can be divided into two basic kinds. They are either thermoset or thermoplastic. Thermoset, when hardened retain their shape. Thermoplastic become soft when heated and return to their original form.

The oldest form of plastic as we know it was demonstrated by Alexander Parkes at the London Exposition in 1862. It was a material derived from cellulose. He called it Parkesine.

John Wesley Hyatt invented Celluloid in 1868. It also was derived from cellulose. He was trying to develop a new material for billiard balls instead of the ivory which was being used at that time to the chagrin of the elephants. He spilled a bottle of collodion on the cellulose and it became a tough flexible film, celluloid. He added camphor to the mixture and it became hard enough to be formed into billiard balls. Mr. Hyatt created celluloid in a strip form for movie film. By 1900 it was an accelerant for the new entertainment form, moving pictures.

PVC, polyvinyl chloride, was invented by Eugene Baumann in 1872.

Casein plastics, milk protein mixed with formaldehyde, were invented in 1897.

A British patent #16,275 was issued in 1899 to Arthur Smith for a phenol-formaldehyde resin plastic. However, it was 1907 when Leo Hendrik Baekeland was successful in improving the phenol-formaldehyde resin plastic. He began to manufacture it commercially under the trade name Bakelite.

The development of various forms of plastic continued throughout the 20th century. Saran in 1933. Polyurethanes in

1937. Teflon in 1938. Nylon and neoprene in 1939. Polyester in 1942. Polypropylene in 1951. Styrofoam in 1954. Thermoplastic Polyester in 1970 under the trade names Dacron, Mylar, Melinix, Teijin and Teteron.

Many of the items in this compilation of The World's 100 Greatest Inventions That Weigh Less Than 16 Ounces are items made from one of these plastics. Is the invention of plastic the Number One invention in the history of the world or is it creating a monstrous litter problem whose detritus will still be with us five hundred years from now?

50. Pop-a-top

In olden days, the 1940's and 50's, to open one of those new-fangled aluminum cans holding your beer, you had to carry a small lever apparatus with a sharp pointed end. That apparatus was often humorously called a 'church key'. You'd punch two holes opposite each other on the top of the can. One would be for air. The other you would drink from. Most of the time you'd drink from the one with the larger hole, of course you would, you are thirsty. One of the most frustrating occurrences in those days was having one or several beers and not having the 'church key' opener. An enterprising young man named Ermal Frase came to the rescue in 1959. He designed a grooved tab with an attached ring on the top of the can. You pulled the ring and the tab came off allowing you to consume the golden beverage. Alright, it could be it wasn't the golden beverage. The pull-tab was also used on soft drink cans. The majority percentage says it *was* the golden beverage.

These pull tabs were very popular but created a litter problem and a safety problem. Barefoot people would step on the discarded tabs and cut their foot.

In 1975 Mr. Daniel Cudzik of the Reynolds Metals Company invented the tab that left the tab on the can.

51. Safety pins

These little items elicited cries of joy from millions of babies instead of just eliciting cries. Before the invention of the safety pin, some baby diapers were held in place with straight pins. Ouch. Most of them were held in place with buttons or ties sewn onto them. Walter Hunt invented the safety pin about 1850. Diapers were held in place with safety pins for a century until man-made diapers of paper and plastic were invented the middle of the 20ᵗʰ century. Now, Velcro is used for that purpose. Safety pins have not become obsolete. They are still used for a multitude of tasks including securing cloth diapers.

52. Screw on bottle caps

What the pop-a-top did for beer and soft drink cans, the screw on cap did for bottles. It was always necessary to have an 'opener' to remove the manufacturer's cap from beer and soft drink bottles. An 'opener' is still necessary today for some beer bottles. Usually the ones from smaller breweries, require it. Those openers are no more the simple "church key". Openers have become another advertising tool with ceramic, glass or plastic handles emblazoned with the logo or name of a company. A French company, Le Bourcharge Mechanique, patented a screw on/ twist off cap in 1959. They discovered the cap was corrosive to alcohol and not marketable. They could have researched the quest for a screw-on bottle cap. They would have discovered that Dan Rynalds, an Englishman, had received a patent in the 1890's for a screw-on cap. Mr' Rynalds cap was also not marketable because it was alcohol corrosive. Le

Bourcharge Mechaniqueand made improvements to eliminate the problem. That cap was impervious to alcohol and solved the problem. U. S. patent #3,930,588 was issued to M. Henri Coursant on Jan. 6, 1976 for a screw-on bottle cap.

53. String (twine, cord, rope)

This item includes all the variations of the basic process comprising string. String is single strands of fiber braided together to form a product with much more strength than is in the individual fibers. The process is the same for cord, twine and rope. String, cord, twine and rope have been in existence for thousands of years. The first use of the process was, supposedly, when prehistoric man discovered that if the vines were twisted together they were much stronger than single vines. This practice has been used even into the twentieth century when Tarzan was able to swing through the jungle on vines, emitting his chilling war cry. String, and all its cousins, are intrinsic in their value and use. We use string and twine to wrap packages. We use cord to open and close blinds and draperies and where would we be today if there were no ropes to control the sails of the ships that took us here, wherever we are. String, twine and cord are relatively light in weight. It takes long lengths to arrive at 16 ounces. Rope is manufactured in many different thicknesses. There are ropes that are twelve feet long before weighing 16 ounces and there are ropes that weigh 16 ounces per lineal foot. The latter half of the twentieth century saw the introduction of fiberglass rope which is much stronger than the fiber ropes before it. Tarzan could have used it to swing through the jungle but, like money, fiberglass doesn't grow on trees.

54. Switch

This is one of the many words in the English language that have multiple meanings. There is switch trains, switch jobs and a slender rod or tree branch used for hitting a person. It was usually a young person being disciplined. The use of the word *was* is intentional. That form of disciplined has been supplanted by other, not as physical methods, time outs, restrictions on television time, denial of social plans, etc. The switching in this item is not of jobs or trains or spanking. It is none of those. This is the simple device initiating the contact between two points and allowing the electric current to flow through it to allow a light bulb to light or a motor to start. John Holmes invented an arc light switch In 1884. William Newton invented the toggle switch in 1897. The light bulb would not be able to shine its light on the world if not for the switch. Think about it. Where would you be without the switch to turn on the light? That's right, in the dark.

55. Velcro®

This simple hook and loop device is an item man survived without for thousands of years. It is now used to replace buttons and zippers. It receives the gratitude of little fingers, elderly fingers and mothers everywhere. Thank you, George de Mestral, the inventor. Monsieur de Menstral, a Swiss engineer, was walking through the woods one day when he noticed the burrs and brambles sticking to his clothing. He looked closely at them and found them to have a hook on them that was catching on the loops in the fabric of his clothes. It gave him the inspiration to invent his new fastening method. .That walk in the woods occurred in 1941. He enlisted the help of friends in the weaving business and in 1955 he was issued a patent for his hook and loop fastener. However, it was not until 1968, with the impetus of Velcro being used in NASA's space suits, that it became popular. It is now in worldwide use on many clothing items and shoes.

56. Water bottle (16.9 oz.)

These plastic bottles filled with water are the constant companion of many. As you know, they weigh 16.9 ounces when filled with water. The explanatory note "Things you need to know" on Page 5 states "No food or drink". Note No. 6 states it also must be "a manufactured or man-made item". The bottle is manufactured. The water is not.

Though, as stated above, they are the constant companion of many, they have presented us with a major problem. The proliferation of plastic beverage bottles has become a major waste issue. According to National Geographic one million plastic beverage bottles are sold in the world every minute. A maximum of 10 percent of the ones sold in the United States are recycled. World-wide it is closer to five percent. We have all heard the stories of the amount of plastic waste finding its way into the seas and oceans endangering marine life. It is estimated to be nine million tons per year.

57. Wristwatch

The thing we don't have enough of is time. We're all slaves to time for no matter what we do, we're getting older every day. To use the time we have efficiently, we have always wanted to know if we have enough time to get there, do that, finish it, meet them, eat, sleep, play and work. To help organize those things, we have invented devices to inform us of how much of the day remains to accomplish what needs to be done. The first such device was the sundial. It was suitable for its purpose if we ignore one important fact. It is a sundial requiring the sun to cast a shadow indicating the time. It, of course, was ineffective at night. Times changed, and the watchman came into being. He would walk the streets and announce the time. He couldn't be on all the streets at the same time leaving some citizens to wonder how much time has passed since the watchman was here and am I going to be late for work again. A need arose to have more accurate information regarding the time. Some portable device was needed that a person could carry with them to know the time. A device was made to accomplish that purpose. It was called a watch in honor of the watchman, who of course lost his job because of it. The device was a large, globular object initially but became smaller over the years until it was capable of being carried in your pocket. Not surprisingly, it was called a pocket watch. Pocket watches began to be made in the 16th century. They were only carried by men, wealthy men. Women thought it another instance of male chauvinism. The women didn't have pockets in which to carry the watches. To soothe the angry and disgruntled ladies, watches were developed in the 17th and 18th centuries as bracelets. They were used exclusively by women as men thought them too effeminate. That thinking changed in the late 19th century when men realized it was much easier to look at a wristwatch when riding a horse than to fish in your pocket for a pocket watch.

Wearing a wristwatch has become unusual for the recent generations. Those persons born in the 1970's, 1980's and later have grown up with the cell phone as an essential part of their everyday attire. They don't need a wristwatch to know the time. Most cell phones display the time as soon as they are turned on.

Wristwatches are still available if you wish to buy one. Some persons are eager to have the status symbol implied from their ownership of a Rolex. After all, the cheapest model is six thousand dollars. A more sophisticated one is twenty thousand unless you want it encrusted with jewels. That price depends on the cost of the jewels you selected.

58. Zippers

We think the zipper is a modern innovation. However, Elias Howe, inventor of the sewing machine, invented a fastener in 1851 that used mechanical means to hold together two pieces of cloth. He called it "An Automatic Continuous Clothing Closure". He was too busy getting his sewing machine produced to devote much time to it. Then, in 1893, Whitcomb Judson patented a device to hold two pieces of cloth together. He called it a "Clasp Locker. Judson established a company called The Universal Fastener Company to manufacture the product. It met with meager success even after being displayed at The Chicago World's Fair in 1895. Gideon Sundback, a Swedish born engineer and an employee of the Universal Fastener Company, made modifications to the device improving its performance and making it saleable. A new patent was issued in 1917 for a "Separable Fastener". They did not call it a zipper. That distinction belongs to the B. F. Goodrich Company who used that name when they put it on the boots and galoshes they manufactured. That was in 1917, over a hundred years ago. So, is that a long time ago? Should we not think of it as a modern invention.

Office items

59. Abacus

This was an invaluable aide in estimating the amount of stones necessary to build the Great Wall of China. The abacus is a calculating device invented by the computer nerds of ancient China before there were computers. Were these guys ahead of the game or what? The abacus has been replaced by the pocket calculator (That is a calculator that fits in your pocket. It is not a calculator to determine how many pockets you have) and the cell phone which can add, subtract, multiply and divide as well as stream your favorite movie or T.V. show. Almost all historians believe the abacus was invented in China. There are some who believe it came from Mesopotamia between 2000 and 1000 B.C. Mesopotamia was one of the most developed areas in the world at those times. The other was China. Mesopotamia means "between two rivers". The two rivers are the Tigris and the Euphrates. The majority of the area of land in Mesopotamia was in what is now Iraq. Some of it was in Syria. Babylon was a major city in Mesopotamia. It was about 50 miles south of present day Baghdad. Babylon may have had 200,000 residents at its heyday. It was the site of one of the seven wonders of the ancient world, "The Hanging Gardens of Babylon". It was also the site of the Tower of Babel contrary to what some believe is actually the Congress of the United States.

60. Cellophane tape

These thin strips of cellophane in widths of one-quarter inch, one- half inch and three-quarters inch with glue on one side are patented by Richard Drew, an engineer with the 3M Company. He received patent #217,627 in October 1939 for his coated cellophane tape. #M started manufacturing the tape using the name "Scotch Cellulose

Tape". It has been very successful. 3M Company was originally the Minnesota Mining and Manufacturing Company. It was founded in 1902 in Saint Paul, Minnesota. 3M introduced the invisible tape in 1975. When applied to a surface it cannot be seen. The Company sells enough tape annually to encircle the earth 165 times. Mr. Drew is a member of The Inventors Hall of Fame.

The tape comes in a roll in a dispenser, leaving us to ponder, 'how come it sticks to everything except the strip of cellophane that is under it in the dispenser? The dispenser, what about the dispenser?

When the 3M Company originally offered cellophane tape for sale, people would have to scratch the almost invisible end of it away from the roll so they could extract a piece. Sometimes, if a person was fortunate, the previous person using the tape would turn over a bit of what was left on the roll so you would not have to scratch the end loose with your fingernail. Then, when you got a piece of tape away from the roll the appropriate length for your need, you had to have a scissors to cut the tape. Mr. John Borden, who was Scotch Tape sales manager at 3M solved this problem. He designed a tape dispenser that held a roll of tape. The end of the tape was not contacting the remainder of it so the end was available and did not require a search to find it. The dispenser had a cutting edge that allowed the tape to be cut when at the proper length.

61. Checks

These pieces of paper inform someone that if they present it to your Bank, the Bank will take the amount of money specified on the piece of paper from your account and give it to the person whose name is on the piece of paper they presented. It is mind-boggling to think of the difficulty our government would have in approving such an arrangement today. There would be countless meetings and opinions. There would be arguments followed by modifications arriving at no decision. The only decision agreed on by all factions is 'how we can tax it'. The use of checks is becoming more and more rare. The development of electronic banking has enabled people to pay their bills with a few keystrokes on their computers or cell phone.

62. Copies

Through the years there have been many attempts to make copies. It is imperative that both parties of a contract have a copy of the contract, that copies of birth certificates, marriage licenses, death certificates and all important paper have multiples in case one is lost or destroyed. Until the eighteenth century copies were made by an individual laboriously copying the words from a document onto a separate piece of paper using a quill and ink. Both Thomas Jefferson and Benjamin Franklin invented a way to copy writing onto another piece of paper. A basic copy machine was invented by James Watt in 1780. That's the same James Watt best known for inventing the steam engine. Carbon paper was patented by Ralph Wedgewood in 1806. Thomas Edison patented an "Autographic Printing Machine" in 1876. Albert Dick made improvements to Edison's machine in 1887. That was the mimeograph machine. He founded the A. B. Dick Company. It was a major supplier of copy machines and office supplies until 2004. Mr. Chester Carlson is credited with inventing the photocopier in 1937. It is a process known as electron Photography. Carlson could not get a major manufacturer to produce his machine. All thought the initial outlay would be too much. Eventually Battelle Memorial Institute, a non-profit, agreed to help Carlson. They put their technical staff, headed by Roland M. Schaffert, to work on it. They made improvements including a dry ink which they called a toner. They were able to sign an agreement in January of 1947 with a small company named Haloid to manufacture the machines. The first machines went to market in 1949. The first copier was named the XeroX Model A. Success came to Haloid XeroX in 1959 with the introduction of their Model 914. It could copy 9" x 14" legal size documents. They changed their name to just Xerox in 1961. Within five years they had revenue of five hundred million dollars. Xerox is now considered a generic term for copies.

63. Erasers

Although pencils were invented sometime after 1564 when graphite was discovered in England, once a person had written something there was no way to correct any misspellings, contradictions or errors. Mr. Edward Naime, an English engineer, picked up a piece of gum elastic and discovered that a person could rub it across pencil markings and it would erase them. He made his discovery in 1770 and started selling "rubber erasers". He used the word rubber as a derivative of the action of rubbing. There was a problem with Mr. Naime's rubber eraser. It crumbled when used and did not last long. Though the erasers did not last, the name "rubber" did. It was not called a rubber tree by the Peruvian natives. It was called arbol del caucho and latex was called caucho. The problem with the short life-span of the "rubber" changed in 1839 when Charles Goodyear invented vulcanization. In 1858 a man named Hymen Lipman, who owned a stationery store, not a brick and mortar place situated on one particular piece of land but a store that sold paper and such, patented a pencil with a piece of rubber attached to one end of it. He sold the patent to Joseph Reckendorfer for $100,000, about two million in today's dollars. The Supreme Court ruled in 1875 that the rubber tipped pencil was not an invention. Therefore, any pencil manufacturer could put rubber tips on their pencils without having to pay a royalty. Of course they did. Arthur Dremel of Racine Wisconsin invented the electric eraser in 1932. It was a shaft of rubber spinning in a rotary tool. It was similar to the other rotary tools of the Dremel Company.

64. Paper

Writing on stone tablets, as it was done in biblical times was very arduous and dirty. Chip a letter, blow the dust out, chip another letter, blow the dust out, etc. Man, in his infinite wisdom, decided there must be a better way. He took the pith and stems of a papyrus bush and smoothed them into sheets and used that to write upon. The papyrus bush is not native to many countries. There had to be a way to make messaging easier. Thankfully, by about 100 BCE, a Chinese man named Ts'ai Lun developed a material that could be written on. It was comprised of bark and hemp and pieces of cloth which he soaked, pressed the water from and let dry There is no more historical information on Ts'ai Lun so we don't know definitely if he was the inventor of paper. We do know that paper as we know it was invented in China. To honor its poor, no longer needed cousin, papyrus, it was called 'paper'.

The Song dynasty (960-1279) was the first to print paper money. The crusades were instrumental in bringing paper technology to Europe. The first paper mill in Europe was in Spain around 1150. France had one by 1190 and Italy had two by 1276. John Tate built the first paper mill in England about 1490. The first paper mill in the United States was built in Pennsylvania in 1690. Prior to then England had been supplying all the paper for the U. S. They had been making paper since the 15th century.

Paper was being made from cloth fibers until the 1830's and 1840's when two men an ocean apart, Friedrich Keller in Germany and Charles Fenerty in Canada, were devoting much time and energy into transforming wood chips into thin pieces of material capable of being written upon, drawn upon and folded without breaking. In 1844 they announced the invention of a machine to extract fibers from wood and make paper from them. Keller and a man named Heinrich Voelter, a German papermaker, were granted a patent for the wood-cut machine in 1845.

Paper is the basis for cardstock, cardboard, poster board and more. Much of it comes from recycled paper. Thirty-six percent of the paper items you see today are made of recycled paper.

65. Paper clips

The modern paper clip was invented by William Middlebrook in 1899. It has not changed nor have there been new, improved versions of the same clip in the one hundred and twenty years since its invention. There have been other paper clip designs before and after Mr. Middlebrook's. There was the Fay clip from 1867, the Wright clip from 1877, the Ridged clip from 1921, the gothic clip from 1933 and the Niagara clip. None have attained the popularity of the Middlebrook clip, a simple design with two opposing loops of wire. So, can we say he put it all together?

66. Pencils

The pencil is an outgrowth of the Romans use of a stylus, a thin lead, to write on papyrus. When man stopped chipping messages onto stone tablets and started using papyrus to write on, it was necessary to find a different method of writing. The chisel they used for chiseling letters into the stone tore holes in the papyrus. The Romans used a stylus, which is a thin lead with a rounded tip that scratches faint letters onto the papyrus. They had to find another way to write. The writing with the papyrus and stylus was not dark enough for those Romans classified as Ancient Romans (over 40) to read. The other way they found was to use the tailfeathers of birds to replace the stylus. They called them quills. They at first tried dipping a quill in berry juice and writing with it. There were several problems with that solution. One, berries were not available in the winter. Two, the sugar in the berries made the papyrus pages stick together. Three, the juice took a long time to dry, it had to evaporate. There were no blow-dryers at that time. They tried ink next and used it successfully for centuries. However, once the ink is put on the paper, (through the centuries papyrus had been replaced with paper), it is indelible, not inedible, (although it is that too). If mistakes are made in the writing, they are there forever. (there is a rumor circulated throughout the centuries that priests were to celebrate, not celibate, a simple clerical error with monumental consequences). Another problem with the pen and quill method, it was difficult to carry ink with you. If your ink bottle is not corked properly, it will spill. It was bad enough that when you put a quill with ink still on it in your breast pocket it left indelible stains on your shirt. This was before the advent of the pocket protector. Lead was used for writing until after graphite was discovered in England in1564. Scientists, or someone, discovered graphite could be used to write with. It leaves a darker mark on the paper than lead. Although graphite is very soft and brittle. So they wrapped it in wood and called it a pencil. That's pen with cil added. Cil being a Neanderthal word meaning 'it's almost like it but it's different'. The first mass-produced pencils were made in Nuremberg, Germany in 1622. There are many German Companies in the pencil making business, Faber-Castell, Lyra, Steadtler and others. The first American made manufacturer was William Monroe of Concord, Massachusetts. He is credited with making the first ones in 1812. William David Thoreau, the author, was also well-known for his pencil making ability. The American pencil industry blossomed in the Industrial Revolution of the 19th Century. Soon, the German manufacturers opened factories in the U. S. Many of the factories had been built in Tennessee due to the availability of the Eastern Red Cedar tree needed for the pencils. Many pencils are now made using Incense Cedar from the California area. The trees are being replaced by what is known as "Sustained yield" where they plant more than they harvest. Pencils are made in a hexagonal shape to prevent them from rolling off your desk. They are painted yellow to indicate they are made with Chinese graphite which is supposed to be stronger. Maybe the graphite is Chinese, maybe it isn't, only the manufacturer knows.

67. Pencil sharpener

When the pencil had been invented, it was a piece of graphite wrapped in wood. It was impossible to write with the pencil. It was covered with wood. It was imperative that the wood be removed exposing the graphite. There was a suggestion made that a knife (not of the table variety but of the honed variety) be included with every box of pencils. The suggestion was tabled for further discussion after someone questioned the wisdom in giving each schoolchild a knife. Instead, the makers of the pencils agreed to provide the pencils with the graphite exposed on one end. Further exposure of the graphite would be the responsibility of the buyer of the pencils. This solved the problem for the manufacturers but the problem remained. How does a person use the rest of the pencil when it is encased in wood? The pencil sharpener answers that question. A Frenchman, Bernard Lassimone got a patent #2444 for a pencil sharpener in 1828. Another Frenchman, Thierry des Estwaux. had another in 1844. It was a hand-held sharpener with a blade fixed inside it. It's similar to what is available today. Eureka Company filed for a patent on a pencil sharpener in the 1860's. John Lee Love, a black inventor, patented a portable pencil sharpener in 1897. It was patent #594,114. The sharpener would sit on a desk and could be decorated or moved. Similar designs are used today. The Boston Pencil Sharpener Company was founded in 1899. In 1913 they introduced the Boston Pencil Pointer. You would insert a pencil in a hole on one side of the sharpener and turn a crank on the other side while holding the pencil so it wouldn't turn. It was a design modified later into the KS model which was screwed to the wall in millions of classrooms so the children could sharpen their own pencils. Teacher's had to empty the shavings reservoir. Electric pencil sharpeners became available to the public in the 1940's.

68. Pens (ball point)

This is the second generation of pen design. It's the third generation if we consider the quill the first. The pen of the first generation, not referring to the quill, but to the fountain pen which was full of ink and not particular as to what surface it would apply its ink. The tip of the fountain pen permitted the ink to run freely from its reservoir inside the pen to any surface the tip touched. It ruined many pockets with its indelible stain. Something had to be done. Laszlo Jozsef Biro was issued a patent in Paris in 1938 for a ball point pen. It had a little ball in the end of it. The little ball rolled around and distributed the ink where it was supposed to be and when it was supposed to be. Laszlo Biro was born in Budapest in 1899. Biro emigrated to Argentina. That's where he started selling his pens. He was not the first to invent a ball point pen. John Loud invented one in 1888 but it was not commercially successful. Mr. Biro's pen attained more success although it tended to leak around the top. The pens were quite expensive, what would be $85 today. People returned them demanding a refund. It was on the verge of bankrupting Mr. Biro when Baron Marcel Bich bought the European rights to manufacture and sell the pens. He paid $2,000,000 for the rights. Baron Bich owned a factory in Clichy, France in which he was manufacturing fountain pens. He altered some machines and purchased others so he could manufacture ball point pens. He solved the problem with the leakage and introduced his ball point pen in 1950. He started selling them through his company, Societe Bic. He had eliminated the H from his name because of the difficulty people had in pronouncing it. Some thought B I C H rhymed with rich. He was very astute in economics and knew his manufacturing costs would permit him to make his pens for 18 cents. They were an instant success. By 1953 he had sold forty million pens. The pens are now available worldwide. Bic Company sold seven billion in 2017. Gone are the days when ink stains destroyed pockets. It was a thing of the past. It no longer happens if the person using the pen remembers to put the cap on the end of the pen.

69. Pens (fountain)

This writing instrument was the writing instrument of choice ever since it was invented. The choices were limited to the fountain pen or the quill. The quill, which is a bird feather, couldn't contain much ink so it was always 'write one or two letters and dip your quill into the ink well to get more ink'. The invention of the fountain pen, which carried its own supply of ink, eliminated the constant dipping of the quill. Mr. Lewis Waterman was an insurance broker. He became very upset when an ink well was spilled on a contract he was negotiating requiring him to rewrite the entire piece. He thought there must be a better way to write than with a quill pen. Waterman started experimenting with ideas for having a pen that contained its own supply of ink. His experiments occupied so much of his time he was fired from his job as an insurance broker. He was not terribly disappointed as he could then continue his experiments. He did so and in 1884 Mr. Lewis Waterman invented the fountain pen. He patented it February 12, 1884. He founded the Waterman Pen Company. By 1901 they were selling 1000 pens a day. They were a well-made product with a no questions asked guarantee. They dominated the market that was soon joined by other makers of pens, Parker, Schaeffer and Eversharp. The Waterman Pen Company in Seymour, Connecticut was acquired by the Bic Company in 1958. Bic needed a factory in the United States to manufacture their ball point pens. The sale of ball point pens had decimated the Waterman Company. Bic offered to purchase sixty percent of the company for a million dollars. Bic got the remaining forty percent for nothing when the true financial picture of Waterman's Company was discovered. Bic moved the factory to Milford, Connecticut. It is now one of several of their factories in the western hemisphere.

70. Postage stamps

Before the advent of computer communications, a person would write a letter to someone using a sheet of paper and a pen It is not enough to write it, it had to be delivered to the addressee. In the days of the quill pen this was done by couriers on horseback. Couriers are expensive and not everyone can afford to have their own courier. Our government vowed to eliminate that problem as it has eliminated all our other problems. The government sells, at a relatively small cost, little pieces of paper with glue on one surface of them. The other surface of the little piece of paper is printed with images of people, places or things the government wants to honor. Surprisingly not all of them are politicians. These little pieces of paper are to be affixed to the letter in the top right corner of the envelope containing the letter. That little piece of paper is assurance that the government takes responsibility for delivering the letter to the person intended. You would deposit the letter in a collection box or take it to the post office. The letter would be gathered together with other letters and entrusted to the care of a courier employed by the government to deliver it, thereby spreading the cost of delivery over the cost of many letters. That courier is known as a postman (or postwoman or post person as the case may be). Until 1974 the glue on the stamps had to be moistened by the sender, either by licking them or swiping them across a damp sponge. !974 saw the introduction of the first self-adhesive stamps. However, the adhesive discolored the stamps and it was discontinued until 1985 when the problem had been solved and the USPS started selling self-adhesive stamps. The post office had become the United States Postal Service (USPS)in 1975. The cost of postage varied depending on time and distance for the first eight decades of the United States. After the entire country was united by the transcontinental railroad in 1869 flat rates were established regardless of time and distance. The rate for a one ounce letter was six cents. It was three cents for a half ounce. Those rates were reduced to four cents and two cents in 1883. On July 1, 1885 they went to two cents an ounce and stayed there until 1917 when it was increased to three cents. That is equivalent to what would be sixty-five cents today. First class postage is currently fifty-five cents an ounce .

71. Rubber bands

When multiple letters are addressed to multiple persons, it is most efficient to gather them and bind them together. They tend to become unruly and slip out of your grasp if left alone. Some means is required to bind them together. Fortunately, we have the rubber tree which provides latex to be vulcanized (the process of vulcanization was discovered by Charles Goodyear in 1839). Vulcanizing solidifies the latex, which is a liquid. It makes it elastic. Thin strips of the elastic rubber are looped to form a circle or band. Thereby creating a 'rubber band'. There was a patent issued in England to Matthew Perry in 1845 for a loop of rubber.

It was not vulcanized and too soon fell apart. Almost eighty years later, 1923, Mr. William Spencer of Alliance, Ohio acquired some innertubes (innertubes were soft, pliable rubber tubes that fit inside automotive tires. Hence the name innertube. Tires nowadays are tubeless). Mr. Spencer got the innertubes from the Goodyear Tire Company of nearby Akron, Ohio. Mr. Spencer cut the innertubes into thin rubber strips and began selling his "rubber bands". He was so successful that he opened a factory in Alliance in 1933. The business did very well selling rubber bands and other rubber products. He moved the factory to Hot Springs, Arkansas in1944. It is still there. The Alliance Rubber Company, 210 Carpenter Dam Road, manufacturing and selling 14 or 15 million pounds of rubber bands annually.

72. Scissors

Scissors are an ancient item invented somewhere around the Middle East. Some say they were invented by Delilah when she wanted to cut Samson's hair while he slept. She was afraid it would pull at his hair too much and wake him if she tried to do it with a knife. He'd be angry and you don't want to make the strongest man in the world angry. This was long before 1977 when David Banner became the Incredible Hulk when he was angry. Delilah needed something that would provide a smoother cut. So she had the local bronzesmith fashion a pair of knives held together at a pivot point so that when the cutting edge of the blades came together they would shear whatever came between them. Even today, one of the main tools of hair cutting and styling is the scissors. Delilah put Samson in prison for a long, long time. His hair grew out and he got his revenge.

Historians say scissors were invented in Mesopotamia in 4000 BCE *or maybe* in Egypt about 1500 BCE. There is no definitive answer as to who invented them.

There is also a great deal of mystery involving the invention of the scissors other than who invented them. The mystery that has perplexed linguists for many years is "why is there a 'c' as the second letter". It would be pronounced the same without this silent letter, scissors or sissors, so why? Why? Why? Perhaps it was one of those indelible errors of ancient times similar to the one mentioned for Pencils.

4

73. Slide rule

This little item was the proud possession of engineers and mathematicians for ages. It always occupied a position front and center in their pocket protector. The slide rule has been around for four hundred years. It was invented by William Oughtred in 1622. It uses two logarithmic scales sliding by one another to do multiplication and division. John Napier had the idea of logarithms and Edmund Gunter created the logarithmic scales about 1620. Variations of the slide rule were made by Henry Coggeshall in 1677, Peter Roget in 1815 and others.

The sliding scales of the piece gave the user instant answers to mathematical calculations. They were used until about 1974 when electric calculators came into being. An electric calculator could provide answers for addition, subtraction, multiplication and division. Now we have the Smart phone which can give you those answers as well as tell you the time and the weather forecast and remind you to bring home milk.

74. Sticky notes

These little pieces of paper are the reminders to children to do their chores and their homework before going out to play. They are posted on the refrigerator by parents everywhere as a gentle reminder of what was told to them three times before they left for school. Parents know it is possible for a child to forget being told three times before school. They have a lot filling their heads before school. Their brain is overloaded with thoughts of friends, used to be friends, rumors, gossip and, once in a while, classes.

The invention of sticky notes is one of those fortunate accidents which turns beneficial. Dr. Spencer Silver, who had a Doctor-of-Science in chemistry degree, was trying to devise a formula for a superior strength adhesive in 1968. Dr. Silver was an employee of 3M Company. Instead of a superior strength adhesive, he found an adhesive which had a very low amount of adhesiveness. The adhesive could be put on a strip of paper and the paper could be moved to a different location without losing its adhesiveness. Dr. Silver tried for years to get 3M management to realize the potential of his low adhesive product. He received encouragement and assistance from the experiments establishing a viable use of the low-tack adhesive from Arthur Fry, another 3M employee, and together they were able to convince 3M management of the potential. Post-it notes were released to national distribution in 1980. Mr. Fry is a member of the Inventors Hall of Fame. Dr. Silver is not.

Personal items

75. Baby bottles

Oh the tragedy of those new mothers who couldn't nurse their baby. They would have to engage the services of a wet nurse to suckle the child. Engaging a wet nurse was expensive. Babies want to eat several times a day and the wet nurse had to be available. The infant mortality rate increased dramatically because too many parents were unable to afford a wet nurse. There was often cow or goat milk available for the baby, as at the time the world was an agrarian society.

The problem, most often, was not being able to have a suitable container for the cow's or goat's milk which was available. Various containers of porcelain and pewter were available until the twentieth century for feeding babies. Those containers had a spout for the baby to drink the milk. The spout was an integral part of the container and was not flexible, which allowed the milk to dribble down the chin of the baby and soil the baby's brand-new party dress. Those porcelain and pewter containers became obsolete when the Pyrex® glass baby bottle with the rubber nipple was introduced in the twentieth century. The Pyrex® bottles were heat resistant and could be used to warm the baby's food. Infant cereal and powdered milk became available for those not having a cow or goat. Baby food formulas were developed specifically for baby bottles. Baby bottles are now made of plastic. The nipples are silicone. The babies don't care what they're made of as long as there's food in it.

76. Diapers (not the cloth ones)

Until recently, 70 years more or less, babies bottoms were covered by cloth squares, folded into a triangle, and secured on the sides by safety pins. These have been supplanted by manufactured diapers of paper and plastic held securely in place by hook and loop fasteners. (Velcro). They are much more convenient and also much more expensive than cloth diapers. Cloth diapers can be washed and reused. Manufactured diapers are not reusable. They're down and out at the count of number two. Cloth diapers are not included in this book because they can weigh more than 16 ounces before use. They can definitely weigh more than 16 ounces after use. Depending on diet and frequency of use by the baby, your child's diaper, the paper and plastic manufactured one, may weigh more than 16 ounces after use, consider yourself warned.

77. Safety razor

Perhaps you have noticed the preponderance of men with beards in the depictions of men in biblical times. You may also see the prevalence of beards on men in photographs taken before the twentieth century. There is a very simple explanation for the popularity of beards in those times. It was difficult, and often painful, to shave. Men visited barbershops weekly to get a shave without cuts and nicks, after suffering through their own daily attempts to shave without injury. Those weekly trips did promote the start of barbershop quartets as the same men would gather there at the same time on a weekly basis. That's a good thing, right? Shaving yourself was a bad thing. Let's cut to the start of the twentieth century when King C. Gillette started selling his safety razor just in the nick of time to prevent more blood-shed. The thin steel blade was enclosed in a case exposing only the cutting edge of the blade. The appearance of clean- shaven men became the norm for more than the first half of the twentieth century. Trimmed mustaches were viewed favorably as it indicated the man was a sophisticated, debonair type of individual regardless of whether he was either.

The Gillette Safety Razor dominated the market until 1975 when Baron Marcel Bich decided he needed another product that was used every day by everyone. It had to be something that would be as successful as his Bic ball point pen. He started manufacturing and selling the Bic disposable razor. It was cheap and he ignored the fact that women did not use a razor every day. It came in a bag of several razors supposably so you could use a new one daily. The Bic disposable razor was another instant success. 2.6 billion were sold in 2016.

78. Sanitary napkins

The condition called the "curse" by women throughout the world was alleviated somewhat by the invention of these fabric pads. Prior to their invention women had used various methods and items to manage their monthly problem. Women used cotton, rags, sheep's wool, knitted pads, rabbit fur and even grass. The first commercially available pad was the Southball pad in 1888. In 1896 Johnson & Johnson marketed a pad with the name Lister's Sanitary Towel for Women. Women were embarrassed to be asking for it so in the 1920's the name was changed to Nupak. The first modern pads to control bleeding were originally used for an entirely different purpose. They were pads to stop the bleeding of wounded soldiers in World War I. The battlefield nurses in France used pads made of wood pulp to stop the bleeding. They were very absorbent. Kotex started selling pads made of cellulose fibers from wood pulp in 1920. They were sold by Kimberly-Clark Company. The company had been in the paper manufacturing business since the 1870's and

4

was looking for a new purpose for the
Cellucotton they had left over from using it
to make bandages for the First World War.
The ad for Kotex from that time says they
are five cents each, 12 for sixty cents. Those
pads had to have a special belt device to
wear them. It hooked the pad in front and
rear to keep it in place. It didn't keep it in
place very well and in the early 1970's
adhesive pads were sold that were affixed to
the underwear.

Tampons first reported use was found in
medical records in ancient Egypt In the fifth
century B.C. Greek women used a
combination of lint wrapped around a small
stick to control the monthly problem. The
Romans used wool. Other cultures used
paper, grass, sponges and cotton. In 1929 Dr.
Earl Haas invented and patented a
compressed cotton tampon as well as an
applicator for it. The tampon had a string
attached for easy removal. The applicator
allowed the user to apply it without soiling
the cotton or their hands. Dr. Haas sold his
patent to Gertrude Tendrich who formed the
Tampax Company to market it. By 1949 the
ads for Tampax were appearing in fifty
magazines. Another tampon was patented by

Dr. Judith Esser-Mittag, she was a German gynecologist, in the 1940's. It did not require an applicator. She later sold her company to Johnson & Johnson. A word of caution, if it ever weighs over 16 ounces after use, get thee to a doctor, girl. You've got problems.

79. Toilet paper tubes

These little pasteboard cylinders are the basis for one of man-kinds most precious commodities. They spin around dispensing their lily white* product until it is gone. Then, sad to say, we discard them after they've given us their all. However, not all of them are lost forever. Some survive and find another life. All hail, recycle.

Sadly, only a small percentage of toilet paper tubes get recycled. There are seven billion rolls of toilet paper sold in the United States annually. Kimberly -Clark, the manufacturers of Scott toilet paper, say they sell 17 billion rolls a year. They sell world-wide. If the 17 billion little 3 3/4 inch long tubes were laid end to end they would be 860,000 miles long. That is almost enough to get to the moon and back, *twice.* Kimberly-Clark has tried to eliminate the toilet paper tube with limited success.

The toilet paper in use today is based on the design patented by Mr. Seth Wheeler in 1891. Mr. Wheeler's patent #465588A was for perforated paper sheets in a roll. Mr. Wheeler's patent application shows the paper hanging over the top, not dangling behind it. That fact will presumably never end the ongoing arguments of over or under of opinionated individuals.

Paper technology has continued to improve the softness and absorbency of toilet paper. It is a far cry from what people had to use before now. They have used rags, grass, corn cobs, leaves and it was the primary reason people waited anxiously for their copy of the latest Sears Catalog.

*The product was manufactured in various colors in the middle of the 20th century. It was discontinued when it was discovered the colors clashed with brown.

80. Toothbrush

Invented by a British gentleman when he still had some of the figgy pudding from Christmas stuck on his teeth the day after Epiphany. He needed something smaller than his finger to get it off. He got the small brush used to remove the grit and grime from the grout in his bathroom tile and used it to clean his teeth. There was a bitter taste to it so he purchased another of the small brushes to use exclusively for his teeth. Maybe that doesn't qualify him as being the inventor of the toothbrush but we can applaud him for his ingenuity in repurposing the tile-brush into a toothbrush. Over time, the name tile-brush was dropped. Now we know it exclusively as a toothbrush. These small brushes are now used only for teeth, but in an ironic twist of fate, they are used for cleaning the grout in tile when they are too grubby for mouths.

Although the above is total fiction, the first to mass-produce toothbrushes was also an English gentleman. His name is William Addis. Mr. Addis was from Clerkenwald, England and mass-produced toothbrushes around 1780. An American patent, #18,653, was issued to H. N. Wadsworth in 1857. The United States has mass-produced billions of toothbrushes since 1885.

The first electric toothbrush, named Motodent, was sold in 1938. An electric toothbrush with the name Broxodent was sold by the Squibb Company in 1959.

Squibb Company is now Bristol-Myers-Squibb. Until nylon was invented in 1935 by the DuPont Company, the bristles on a toothbrush were boar bristles. Colgate alone, manufacturers 1.4 billion manual and electric toothbrushes per year. There are many other manufacturers.

81. Toothpaste

A misnomer. It should actually be called toothsoap. Toothpaste would be used to fasten loose teeth. Toothpaste was unknown until the start of the 20th century. Prior to then, people used toothpowders to clean their teeth or they used salt or sodium bicarbonate. Dr. Washington Sheffield mixed tooth powder with glycerin to make toothpaste in 1892. He began putting toothpaste in collapsible tubes. His son had seen artists with collapsible tubes for their paints. The doctor adopted the use of that kind of tube for his toothpaste. He called his toothpaste "crème dentifrice". Dr. Sheffield was most likely unaware of his owing a huge debt of gratitude to John Goffe Rand. Mr. Rand invented the collapsible tube. He was issued a patent in 1841 for his "metal rolls for paint". Prior to that time paint had been stored and carried in pig bladders. However, once the bladder was punctured to get to the paint it was impossible to reclose it. This was before the invention of duct tape and cellophane tape. An authentic claim can be made that the invention of the tube is a more worthwhile invention than the toothpaste. Is it? Colgate started selling toothpaste in tubes in 1895. They called theirs "dental ribbon crème" Pepsodent, a toothpaste brand owned by Unilever, a British and Dutch company, achieved immense popularity in the 1930's, 40's and 50's when it began sponsoring radio shows. It sponsored the Amos n Andy Show in the 1930's and the Bob Hope Show in the 40's and 50's. Fluoride became an additive to toothpaste in the 1960's. Pepsodent did not add fluoride to their toothpaste and their sales suffered. As of the start of the 21st century, Colgate, Crest and Gleem share over sixty percent of the market. Pepsodent ranks tenth.

4

Recreation & outdoor items

82. Arrows

There is evidence that the arrow was invented before the bow. Stone points were found in a cave in Subudu, South Africa in 1983. They are believed to be between 60,000 and 65,000 years old. Were they stone points for arrows or spears? We don't know. If they were arrow points, the person would have to walk up to their prey and physically stick the arrow into them. Since it would have been a very dangerous thing to do, maybe it was the inspiration for a bow, where one did not have to be at arm's length to insert the arrow into the prey. Likewise, they made the arrows longer to maintain a distance from their prey. That was the origin of the spear. Arrowheads and pine arrow shafts have been found in the Ahrensburg valley north of Hamburg, Germany dating to 10,000 BCE. The bones of 600 reindeer were found at the same site. Some had arrowheads embedded in the bones. There are cave drawings of 5000 years ago showing bows and arrows being used to hunt deer. The oldest bows were found in a peat bog in Denmark in 1944. They are approximately 9000 years old.

The end of the arrow shaft opposite the arrowhead has two pieces attached to it called fletches. They are affixed to the shaft by glue or embedded in it. They are there to aid in the accuracy of the archer's shot. They prevent the arrow from wobbling in flight. The bow and arrow have been used on every continent except Australia. Whether they were independently invented on each continent is not known, More likely, the idea was brought to them by travelers. The bow and arrow had been a formidable weapon for more than 10,000 years. The accomplished English longbowman could shoot six arrows per minute at his foe. The 16th century of the

Common Era saw firearms replace the bow and arrow as the most effective weapon. Archery is enjoyed by many these days as a recreational or competitive pastime. Archery has been a sport in the modern Olympics since 1900.

83. Balls

Balls weigh more than 16 ounces, don't they? Size 5 soccer balls, those for players older than twelve, weigh from 14.8 to 16 ounces. NFL footballs weigh 14 or 15 ounces and are inflated to 12.5 to 13.5 pounds per square inch (unless you're the New England Patriots). A volley ball weighs slightly less than 10 ounces. Basketball players have the heaviest balls. Basketball players balls weigh 22 ounces so they are excluded from this list. Their balls are too heavy. Many balls aren't nearly 16 ounces. There are baseballs, golf balls, softballs, racquet balls, tennis balls, ping pong balls, Nerf® balls, Wiffle® balls and beach balls. There are also the rubber and plastic balls kids, dogs and cats play with. Playing with balls is not a new pastime nor is it strictly a pastime of the so-called civilized world. The early explorers on the North American continent saw the Mohawk and Seneca Indians playing a game with a small ball in which the players were holding sticks trying to get the ball past their opponents and into an enclosure. This is a game we have adopted and adapted into what we call lacrosse. Lacrosse is becoming a popular sport at the high school and collegiate levels. It is being played by both men and women. There are over 80,000 female lacrosse players in high schools and more than 100,000 men. It is said to be today's fastest growing sport, faster than soccer. It is also said to be the world's fastest moving sport.

84. Barbie doll

The Barbie doll was the invention of Ruth Handler. It was inspired when Ruth saw her daughter, Barbara and her friends, playing with paper dolls for hours. They would dress and undress them in paper cutouts of clothes. Ruth wondered why there were no three dimensional dolls. Why were there no dolls children could hold in their hand and dress in real clothes, not paper cutouts? So she designed one. Ruth had an inside track to get it manufactured as she and her husband, Elliot, were co-founders of the Mattel Toy Manufacturing Company. Elliot and Harold "Matt" Matson had started it in 1945. Mattel was a combination of Matt and El(liot). Due to poor health Matson sold his share to the Handlers in 1947.

The Barbie Doll was introduced to the world at the American Toy Fair in New York City in 1959. The Ken doll was

4

introduced two years later. 300,000 of the dolls were sold the first year. They cost $3.00.

Throughout the years there have been over 180 different outfits for Barbie to wear. All of the outfits depict Barbie in a different profession to show girls they can be anything they want to be even President of the United States. Getting girls to aspire to be what they wanted to be was Ruth Handler's passion. The year's outfit, costing from $1 to $5, were sold based on the latest fashion trends. Over 70 different fashion designers have designed clothes for Barbie.

The Barbie doll is 11.5 inches tall and weighs 7 ¼ 0unces. The doll has been both brunette and blond and in 1961 a red-headed Barbie was introduced. A Hispanic and an African-American Barbie were introduced in 1961.

Mrs. Handler took an active part in the operations of Mattel. Over the years they have acquired the rights, and manufacture some of the world's most successful toys. They have Fisher-Price, Hot Wheels, Matchbox, Masters of the Universe. Polly Pocket, American Girl, Thomas and friends and others. Mrs. Handler, after suffering a mastectomy in 1970, designed a more natural feeling prosthetic. She received a patent on it in 1975 and started producing and selling it under the name Nearly Me. Ruth Handler died on April 27, 2002.

85. Frisbee®

This simple disc of plastic is one of the favorite playthings of man and dogs. It is thrown with a wrist action and sails through the air in a course of its own choosing going left or right from the person who threw it to the catcher on the other end of its course. Whether the catcher be person or dog the Frisbee® doesn't care.

Mr. Walter Morrison invented the item in 1948 after being inspired by college students playing pitch and catch with tin pie plates. The plates were from the Frisbie Company of Bridgeport, Connecticut. Morrison sold the "Pluto Platter" as he called it to the Wham-o Toy Company in 1955. They began selling it with the name Frisbee in 1958. It became a national craze. They had sold over 100 million by 1977.

Realizing its enduring appeal, Mattel Toy Manufacturers bought it from Wham-O in 1994. There are now many variations of the basic pitch and catch game. There is Frisbee Golf, Ultimate Frisbee and Freestyle Frisbee. There are Frisbee contests and competitions for both humans and dogs.

All official contests use the rules and regulations of the World Flying Disc Federation. It is an 85 country alliance. It is an international federation recognized by the International Olympic Committee.

86. Gunpowder

Gunpowder is included as a recreational item in consideration of all the skeet shooters and hunters. It is definitely an outdoor item. It was invented by the Chinese a thousand or so years ago. It is unclear whether the gun was invented first and the Chinese wondered what they could do with it so they invented the gunpowder or whether the gunpowder was invented first and the Chinese wondered what they could do with it so they invented the gun. The Chinese were not selfish with their discovery and the knowledge spread to other parts of the world. A person could ponder the question of 'would the world have been better off if the Chinese had kept the knowledge to themselves or would mankind have found other terrible ways to kill people'.

87. Harmonica

There was a mouth-blown instrument called the Sheng in China BCE. Some accounts credit the harmonica as we know it today to

Christian Friedrich Buschmann of Berlin, Germany in 1821. Buschmann named the instrument 'Aura'. He was 16 years-old in 1821. He played his instrument for people and it became popular although it only gave blow notes. A man named Richter invented the two reed harmonica in 1825. It gave notes for both inhaling and exhaling. Manufacturers began producing it in the mid-19th century. The most well-known was the Hohner Corporation headed by its founder, Matthias Hohner. Hohner introduced the harmonica into the United States in 1862. Harmonicas were imported to Japan in 1896. Nippon Gakki Co. LTD, which later became Yamaha Corporation, began producing harmonicas in 1914. It had a distinctive 'butterfly' logo. They sold them world-wide but ceased production in the 1940's, the WWII years. They resumed in 1945. However, they no longer produce them.

The harmonica has been a tremendous component of 'blues' music. There have been several men who attained celebrity status playing the harmonica. The most famous was Larry Adler who died in 2001. In the 1930's and 1940's there was John Lee "Sonny boy" Williamson, Rice Miller and

Little Walter and of course Bob Dylan plays harmonica.

88. Kites

The Chinese were the inventors of kites. It is only one of the many things they have invented as you know if you've read the preceding pages of this book. The possibilities are endless of all the things they may have invented if they hadn't been so busy making babies as the most populous nation in the world, population 1.4 billion and counting. The earliest account of kite flying in China was about 200 B.C. Kites were introduced to Japan around the 7th century by Buddhist monks. They were used as talismans to avert evil spirits. They were used exclusively by the upper classes until roughly 1600 A.D. when those people lower than the samurai were permitted to use them. In 1712 a man named Kakinoke Kinsuke used a giant kite to fly himself to the top of Nagoya castle. He stole the golden scales from two dolphin figures. Alas, he was captured and boiled in oil. Kites were instrumental in many experiments in understanding electricity and wind currents. We know of Benjamin Franklin's experiment with a kite in a thunderstorm. I'm sure his mother would not have approved of him flying a kite among lightning bolts. The Wright Brothers used a kite to test the design of their flying machine in 1903. Kites were used in World War I to spy on enemy troop positions. The U. S. Weather Service has used kites to elevate meteorological instruments. The study of the actions of kites helped to develop hang gliders and sports parachutes. Kites are used as the means of propelling vehicles over ice, water and land. There is a World Kite Museum in Long Beach, Washington and the American Kitefliers Association in Cedar Ridge, California. Kite flying is enjoyed by many individuals. Which poses the question. If kite flying is supposed to be such a pleasurable experience, why is the expression "go fly a kite" an insult?

89. Legos

A basic interlocking Building Cube was invented by Hillary Fisher Page in 1932. They were issued a British patent, #529580 in 1939. Page made modifications to the design and was issue patent #633055 in 1949 for the Self-Locking Building Bricks. In 1947 Ole Kirk Christiansen, a man from Denmark, was manufacturing small wooden toys as the Lego Group. He obtained samples of Page's Self-Locking plastic blocks. He began producing a modified version of them as Automatic Binding

Bricks. In 1954 Gotfred, Ole's son, as managing director of the company had the idea of making many related toys so customers could build their own cities with the toys. They patented several new designs to eliminate competition. Legos were not always overwhelmingly popular. The company had years in which it lost money. However, it began to manufacture the toy building blocks with licensing agreements featuring fictional heroes and cartoon characters. The release of the movie Star Wars spawned Star Wars Lego. Winnie the Pooh Legos soon followed. Then in 2000 with Lego Harry Potter. It established an agreement with Warner Brothers for The Lego Movie and The Lego Batman Movie. They continue to have a successful collaboration as The Lego Group and Warner Animation Group. Watch for Lego Tom and Jerry at your favorite theater spring 2021.

90. Playing cards

The true origin of playing cards is, as is the case in so many common items, unknown. They may have originated in China during the Tang Dynasty. Between 900 and 1000 A. D. There is some evidence that playing cards were in Europe before then. However, the earliest known written mention was in 1377.

It is in the writings of a monk named Johannes in Switzerland. The playing cards in the first European decks at that time used cups, swords, clubs and coins as the four suits. There is evidence that a deck was 52 cards. The decks had a king, a queen and a knave (jack). The Spanish also had cards. They have a game called Ombre that has a deck of 40 cards. It has a king, a knight and a knave and the numbers 1 through 7. Germany became a major manufacturer of playing cards as their use became more popular having been introduced by traders, gypsies and soldiers. The German decks used acorns, leaves, hearts and bells as the four suits. The four suits that we use today, spades, hearts, diamonds and clubs, were developed by the French early in the fifteenth century. The French are also responsible for a major change in playing cards. They established the use of two colors. Red and black, for the cards. The red for hearts and diamonds, the black for clubs and spades. The preceding statement is not quite accurate. The French suits were coeurs, piques, carreaux and trefles. The reason piques (pikes) was translated to spades and trefles (clover) was translated to clubs is unknown. Perhaps it was because the suits were named spades and clubs in the Italian decks. The first American to manufacture playing cards was Lewis Cohen in 1832. Prior to that time all playing cards had been imported. His business was so successful it became a public company in 1871, The New York Consolidated Card Company. They patented the use of indices, small printing at the corners so a person knew what card it was without having to fan their hand. The U. S. introduced Jokers into the pack in the 1870s. There were several manufacturers of playing cards in the late 19th century. Besides The New York Consolidated, there was Samuel Hart and Company and Russell & Morgan which eventually became the United States Playing Card Company, which is now the major supplier of all the playing cards in the world. They make the Bicycle, Bee and Tally Ho brands. Their Corporate Offices are in Cincinnati, Ohio. Playing cards have been entertaining children and adults for thousands of years. In fact, Jesus told Peter to 'go fish'. Fortunes have been won and lost at the card table. Marriages have been dissolved after a husband or wife trumped their spouse's ace. There are different playing cards for different cultures. They all have the same purpose, to defeat your opponent in such a way that they will be angry, humiliated, broke or broken. You may think that's rather harsh but don't be so sensitive. You'll never win with that attitude.

91 Sunglasses

Sunglasses have been the necessary accessory for movie stars and celebrities for less than a hundred years. Before now, man toiled outdoors for thousands of years before discovering a way he could eliminate some of the glare from the sun in the summer and the equally intense reflection from the snow in the winter by putting a dark film over his eyes. The Eskimos used a piece of whale bone with slits cut into it horizontally to reduce the glare from the snow.

In the 12th century some Chinese tried holding gems in front of their eyes to eliminate glare. There was no widespread use of this method, most of the people didn't have gems.

James Ayscough, he was also mentioned in the eyeglasses category, started to investigate the use of tinted lenses in 1752. In the late 19th century glasses tinted amber or brown were prescribed for people who had syphilis. Their eyes are more sensitive to light. There-fore be careful in choosing the tint of your sunglasses. You don't want to give people the wrong impression. Mass production of inexpensive sunglasses was started in 1929 by Sam Foster. He sold his Foster-Grant sunglasses from a Woolworth store on the boardwalk in Atlantic City. Polarized sunglasses became available in 1936. Ray-Ban developed polarized Aviator glasses for use during the Second World War. Today, most sunglasses have protection against ultra-violet (UV) rays. We can be grateful we have sunglasses when we drive. We can see that car approaching us and not try to pass the car in front of us. Our two cars traveling at sixty miles an hour will each go four hundred forty feet in five seconds. Crash, bang, but officer, I was blinded by the sun you'll be able to tell the officer from your hospital bed if you're lucky enough to be in the hospital.

92. Whistles (not the train kind)

This is one of the most under- appreciated inventions. It is of extreme importance to many groups of people. It is the main communicative device of referees, band directors, coaches and drill sergeants. The sound of their whistle halts all movement until the whistle sounds again. In between the two shrill sounds of the whistle, the referee, band director, coach or drill sergeant has gently explained to his or her charges why the whistle was blown and what he or she wants done or why they have performed incorrectly. The world would be a less orderly place without the kindness and guidance of the referees, band directors, coaches and drill sergeants of the world.

This is another invention we can attribute to the Chinese. The first whistle is supposed to have been 5000 years ago. That would make the whistle older than the abacus, the compass or paper. The whistle it referred to is most likely the fipple flute. A fipple is the small piece of wood inside the whistle mouthpiece that controls the air movement producing the sound. Fipple flutes have been modified to fit various tasks. There are the boatswain's pipe used on board ships. There is the one used on galley ships to keep the strokes. There are the whistles used by military commanders to assemble the soldiers. The first recorded use of a whistle for a sporting event was in 1878. It was at the Nottingham Forrest Soccer Club. The opponents and the score of the match are lost to history. The whistle for sporting events is normally called a "pea" whistle for the little ball inside it, the fipple. A major American manufacturer of whistles is The American Whistle Corporation, 6540 Huntley Road, Columbus, OH 43229. They are the only manufacturer of metal whistles in the United States.

93. Yo-Yo's

The yo-yo has been around for centuries. It is considered the second oldest toy. The doll is first. The yo-yo came to Europe around 1800. It was not called the yo-yo. The British called it bandalore. The French called it l'emigrette. The name yo-yo was brought over from the Philippines by Pedro Flores. Filipinos had been using it for four hundred years. A much larger version was used as a weapon. Pedro Flores emigrated to the U. S. in 1915. He had played with yo-yos as a boy in the Philippines and thought children would love them. Flores began producing yo-yos in a small factory in Santa Barbara, California. He sold 300,000 yo-yo's the first year, 1928. A man named Donald Duncan, who owned the Duncan Toy Company, saw the toy and believed it had enormous possibilities. He bought the rights from Flores in 1929. He trademarked the name "Yo-Yo".

Duncan started producing the Yo-Yo's in a factory in Luck, Wisconsin. Yo-Yo's became a national craze. Duncan's factory was producing 3600 Yo-Yo's an hour. There were three million were sold in Philadelphia alone in 1931. Sales reached their peak in 1962 at 45 million. However advertising and production costs ate away the profits. Duncan sold his name, trademark and all the rights to the Yo-Yo to Flambeau Plastic Company. They continue to produce Yo-Yo's in plastic to this day. They retain the name Duncan Toy Company.

Donald Duncan is also a famous inventor and innovator. He founded the Good Humor mobile ice cream franchise. He is also the inventor of the parking meter and the concept of the "proof of purchase" stamps or box tops to redeem merchandise.

Tools & hardware items

94. Duct tape

The ultimate multi-use invention. Duct tape has come far from its original purpose of being used to wrap the joints in heating ducts therefore preventing the air coming from your furnace or air conditioner to escape before it reaches its planned outlet. That is why it is called duct tape and not 'duck' tape. There have been adhesive tapes for more than a hundred years. None have the popularity or variety of uses of duct tape.

Johnson and Johnson made a cloth backed adhesive tape for the U.S. military in the 1940's which is basically the same as what we use today. Duct tape is used in any instance where things have to be affixed to other things. It has been used to make clothing and kitchenware. It has been used to close the unintended punctures in balls and balloons and vacuum bags. Feel free to add to the list with anything you have used it for.

----

95. Dynamite (stick)

The epitome of small but powerful. One stick of dynamite weighs about ten ounces. Use enough of it and you can move mountains. It's been done many times. Mountains of dirt and rock have been moved by road builders, miners and quarries. It is, stick by stick, a necessary tool of those trades. It has been utilized by others in inglorious ways causing death and destruction. The inventor, Sir Alfred Nobel, was so concerned about that possibility, he established the Nobel Peace Prize to honor the peacekeepers of the world. It is probably unnecessary to tell you 'don't try dynamite at home'.

96. Knives

The first knives would not be eligible for inclusion in this list. They weren't manufactured unless you consider the wisdom of that unknown man who realized the piece of thin rock held in his hand could help in skinning the animal he'd killed for food or to cut vines to braid into rope. Those pieces of thin rock were no longer needed about 3000 B.C. when the bronze age came and man began to fashion knives from metal. Most of the knives of that age were used as weapons and, of course, weighed more than 16 ounces. That is immaterial to this list as explained in note No. 3 of 'Things you need to know' on page No. 5. Almost all the knives we use on a daily basis weigh less than 16 ounces. They are the paring knife, the chopping knife, the chef's knife, the carving knife and the cheese knife. The table knife is listed as part of the Table Service The Table service could also include the butter knife, but it doesn't. Then there is the pocket knife. It could easily have been a part of the Personal Items category as it is carried daily by many people. It is so utilitarian in its uses that it is in the Tools category. Folding knives have been in existence for thousands of years. A folding knife was discovered in the excavation among the ruins of a civilization dating to 600 BCE There is evidence they were carried by soldiers of the Roman Legions. The most famous of the folding knives is the Swiss Army Knife. This multi-tool knife was first produced In 1891. Folding knives have received much criticism and most civilized entities have passed laws limiting the legal length of the blade. The 'switch- blade' knife is the recipient of much of the criticism. The switch-blade knife has a button on it. When the button is pressed, the blade is switched from its place in the handle to being fully exposed. It is extremely handy when you are holding something and need a free hand to cut the something with the knife. That something should not be another person. There are laws prohibiting it.

97. Measurers (tape, rulers, yardsticks, etc.)

This is another very important invention that cannot be attributed to any particular individuals. Will it fit? How big is it? Is it too long? How far is it? These questions are asked, either verbally or mentally, millions of times a day. We have, thanks to these items, some things to turn to which can provide the answer. They come in many different lengths and materials. Almost all of them are thin strips of cloth, metal or plastic with printed markings graduated by inches and feet, or by centimeters and meters for their entire length. The length varies according to the item. A ruler is 12 inches. A yardstick is 36 inches. A tape measure can be various lengths from eight feet to a hundred feet. One of the simplest and lightest weight is the cloth measuring tape used by tailors when they are tailoring. One special measuring device that was used for a very long time is the carpenter's six foot folding rule. That long pocket on the right leg of your blue jeans was designed to carry that folding rule. That loop on the left leg is for your hammer.

Though we currently use inches, feet and yards or millimeters, centimeters and meters as units of measure, it has not always been that way. Noah built the ark measuring it in cubits. The cubit was about 20 inches or 45 centimeters. We no longer measure in cubits. Perhaps we will again, when we build an ark.

98. Nails & screws

The nail is a fascinating invention. It's a piece of wire with one end pointed and the other end flattened. You drive it into a piece of wood by hitting the flattened end with a hammer. (Most hammers, other than tack hammers, weigh more than 16 ounces making them ineligible for this list). Nails have been found in Egyptian ruins dating to 3400 BC. We know Jesus was nailed to the cross 2000 years ago. The nails used for the crucifixion were rough, hand forged nails. There are three types of nails but over 2000 different kinds for different purposes. The three types are forged nails, made by a blacksmith one at a time. There are cut nails and wire nails which are machine made at the rate of thousands per hour. Most of what we use are wire nails of various names. There are common nails, box nails, finish nails, roofing nails, cement coated nails, ring shank nails and double-head nails to name a few. Cut nails are still used for certain things. Oak strip flooring is usually laid using cut nails. Cut nails are a rectangular shape unlike the round shape of wire nails. The rectangular shape gives the nail more gripping surface into the wood. Cut nails are used in boat building. It would not be desirable to have cracks between the boards when you're afloat. Nail sizes are differentiated by the "penny". The more pennies, the longer the nail. Nails range from 2d to 60d. The most common are 3d for trim work and 16d for framing work. A 3d nail is 1 ¼". A 16d is 3 ¼". 60d are 6" long. Where did the term "penny" originate to designate nail size? It is believed to have started because it cost 16 pence (pennies) to buy a hundred nails of that size way back in medieval times. The penny size is represented by the letter "d" (lower case) because it refers to the Latin word for coin "denarius". There are nails shorter than 1". They are called brads and tacks. Nails longer than the 60d are designated by their length in inches. Nails were scarce and expensive in colonial times. People would have a small forge setup at their house and make their own. Thomas Jefferson made nails as one of his hobbies. Maze Nails of Wareham, Massachusetts is still making nails as they have been since 1819. They deliver them in 100 lb. kegs.

Screws are the second part of this item. There are as many sizes and variety in screws as there is in nails. The first screw type device was invented by Archimedes in the 3rd century BCE. It was not a device to hold two pieces together but rather a large screw in a shaft to lift water from a lower to a higher place. The theory of the screw, a device that when being turned exerts torque , was known but the ability to manufacture it was unknown until 1770 when Jesse Ramsden, an English man, invented a screw-cutting lathe. In 1797 Henry Maudslay, another English man, began producing screws. David Wilkinson of the United States started producing them in1798. Those screws had a square head and were inserted with a wrench, Slotted head screws appeared somewhat later. The production of slotted head screws required a device to insert them into the materials to be attached. At first a bit was designed to fit into a carpenter's brace A brace is the tool used to drill holes in material. It is better known as a drill. It is believed that a hand-held screwdriver was first used in the fifteenth century. The screw is of no use without the screwdriver. The screwdriver could be considered as an equally important invention as the screw.

P. L. Robertson of Canada invented and patented what is called a screw with a square drive head in 1908. Over 700 of them were used in the manufacture of each Model T Ford. Robertson's invention was followed by the invention of the Phillips head screw. It was invented by Henry Phillips, an Oregon businessman, in 1936.

William G. Allen of Connecticut invented the Allen screw. It has a hexagonal indentation in the flat head of the screw. A special tool, the Allen wrench, is inserted into the indentation to tighten the screw. e P so the screwdriver was born. They are designed for different purposes. All are to be used to firmly connect two pieces of material. There are basically two types of screws, flat head and round head. Flat head can be screwed into so that the top of it is slightly below the surface of the material. It is countersunk into the material. The head is covered with filler, sanded and painted so the screw is not visible. The round head screw stays atop the material.

Nails may also be depressed into the wood. They must be firmly struck with the hammer to counter-sink them. Then the depression can be filled with putty or spackle, sanded and painted.

A nail makes its own hole in the wood and is expected to stay there. It is not to come out of the hole. It's to grab onto the sides of the hole permanently. You may want to remove a nail at times. Nails are stubborn. They don't want to lose the position into which they've been driven. Considerable force has to be exerted on them to get them out of their hole. Some hammers are made with a claw on the end opposite of the driving surface to facilitate the extraction of those stubborn nails.

Sometimes, if there is too much pressure being put on the nail. It may work its way out of the hole on its own allowing the pieces it was holding together to separate. If that happens, screw it.

99. Sandpaper

A patent for sandpaper was issued to Isaac Fischer of Springfield, Vermont in 1834. That was not the first use of an abrasive material attached to paper. The Chinese were using crushed shells adhered to parchment paper in the 13th century. The sand on sandpaper is not really sand. It is either aluminum oxide or silicon carbon. 3M Company has been using those products for its sandpaper since 1921. The coarseness of sandpaper is defined by the 'grit' number. A 24 grit is very coarse. The grit number can be as high as 1000. That would be an extremely fine grit used for polishing. Fine grit sandpapers are those in the 120 – 220 range. 240, 320 and 400 grit are very fine grit sandpapers.

100. WD-40

This product was developed in 1953 by the Rocket Chemical Company of San Diego, California. The product is the 40th formula developed as a water displacement (the WD) to protect the skin of Convair's Atlas missile from rust and corrosion. It was made available to the public in 1958. It has many uses as a rust inhibitor and lubricant. Rocket Chemical changed their name to WD-40 Company, Inc. and went public in 1973. The company has four manufacturing plants worldwide using the formula which, to this day, remains a trade secret. The company had revenue of 408.5 million dollars in 2020.

4

<u>Honorable mention</u>

There were items in the 1st edition which had interesting stories or background. They are not included in this 2nd edition because of other items deemed more deserving. There are also items that were researched but are not in the book. They deserve mentioning.

Baseball cap

The baseball cap has been around since the 1860s but it was not a piece of regular wearing apparel until the 1970s. The Brooklyn Excelsiors wore a rounded top cap with a button on top of it in 1860. The Excelsiors must have been an amateur baseball team as the Cincinnati Reds, at the time known as the Cincinnati Red Stockings, were the first all professional team. Their first professional game was on May 4, 1869. They defeated the Great Westerns 45 – 9.

Bubble wrap (not in the 1st edition)

This is another of those items requiring many square feet before it totals 16 ounces. Bubble wrap is basically two sheets of plastic fused together in a waffle pattern leaving small air pockets between the seals. The invention was an accidental consequence of an effort by Marc Chavannes and Alfred Fielding in 1957 to create a three-dimensional wallpaper. Bubble wrap is a generic trademark for a product of Sealed Air Corporation.

Clothes hangers

The first of what could be considered a clothes hanger was invented and patented by O. A. North of New Britain, Connecticut in 1869. It was a variation of a wire hook. Thomas Jefferson had an apparatus in the closet in his home, Montecello, for hanging his clothes. It was a series of rotating bars. It is one of the many things Jefferson designed. That was in the 1760s or '70s. The wire hanger we are familiar with today was the idea of Albert J. Parkhouse of Jackson, Michigan in 1903. Mr. Parkhouse was an employee of the Timberlake Wire and Novelty Co. They began manufacturing and selling them. Soon, other companies began manufacturing them. There are now clothes hangers with the top rounded to conform to the shape of people's shoulders. Clothes hangers are now made of wood and plastic as well as wire. There are some people who get very upset if they have to hang their clothes .on wire hangers. A 1981 movie, "Mommie Dearest", has a scene in which the mother gets violently upset because her daughter hung her clothes on wire hangers.

Deodorant

The first commercial deodorant, Mum, was patented in 1888 by an inventor from Philadelphia, Pennsylvania. Bristol – Myers purchased it in 1931. There are two types of deodorants. There is the ordinary deodorant which kills the bacteria that feeds on our sweat thereby eliminating the odor. There is also the anti-perspirant deodorant which blocks the sweat glands from producing sweat. The first deodorant, Mum, was a cream applied to the underarms with your fingers. A deodorant named Everdry was marketed in 1903. It had aluminum oxide as a main ingredient. In the late 1940's Helen Barnett Diserens developed a roll-on deodorant inspired by the design of a ball point pen. Ban, the first roll-on deodorant was introduced in 1952.

Hula Hoop®

The Hula Hoop® was introduced to the public by Arthur Melin and Richard Kneer of the Wham-O Toy Company in 1958. Children had played with hoops for hundreds of years. Those hoops were the rings holding the staves of barrels together. Not all children had a barrel ring available to them. Wham-O Corporation's hoop was the first wide use of high density polyethylene (HDPE) plastic. The plastic tubing hoop was available to everyone in 1958 for the sum of $!.98. They sold twenty-five million of them in four months and over two hundred million of them in two years. Wham-O is located in Carson, California.

Kazoos (not in the 1st edition)

The kazoo was invented in the 1840s. Its first appearance was at the Georgia State Fair in 1852. Legend says it was invented by Alabama Vest, an American black man, and Thaddeus Von Clegg, a German clockmaker. How an American black man and a German clockmaker got together to invent it in the 1840s is a mystery. The kazoo wasn't produced commercially until 1912 when Emil Song and Michael McIntyre, who was a tool and die maker, started making them. McIntyre teamed up with a man named Harry Richardson who owned a big metal factory. They began mass producing kazoos in 1916 under the name of The Original American Kazoo Company. McIntyre got a patent on his design of the kazoo in 1923. The factory is still in existence today and still making kazoos. Next to the original factory is a museum telling the history of the kazoo.

Plastic wrap

A similar purpose to aluminum foil used to wrap leftovers. The difference being the ability to see what is inside and decide you will have it later. Later never comes and eventually you discard it. Plastic wrap is incredibly lightweight. It requires approximately 400 square feet to weigh 16 ounces. That would be enough to wrap one gigantic casserole. The first plastic wrap was Saran wrap. It invention is credited to Ralph Wiley, an employee of Dow Chemical Company. Supposedly he discovered it accidentally in 1933. Mr. Wiley was trying to create a dry cleaning product when he found he could not clean a glass that had contained polyvinylidene chloride. It was coated with a thin plastic film. The product was developed by Dow Chemical as a spray and was used as a protective coating. It was sprayed on fighter aircraft in World War II to reduce the effects of sea water. Dow received approval in 1949 to market it as a film to preserve food. They sold it under the name Saran Wrap. Saran Wrap became the property of S.C. Johnson Company in 1998 when they acquired it from Dow.

Potato peeler

A device used to remove the natural covering of a potato, thereby eliminating 30% of its nutritional value. It is not necessary to remove the covering of the potato. It is edible. It is suggested that you wash them. They grow underground, therefore are dirty when gathered. There are two basic designs of potato peelers. There is the straight peeler and the Y peeler. Both have a double blade attached to a handle. One blade is sharpened to remove the peeling. The other is not sharp to prevent it from digging into the vegetable. The straight potato peeler has been around for a long time. Prior to its invention a paring knife was used for peeling potatoes. Mr. Alfred Neweczeral of Davos, Switzerland invented the most popular Y shape peeler in 1947. It is sold as the Rex Potato Peeler. Though it is called a potato peeler it is equally capable of peeling carrots, apples, pears etc.

Tweezers

The midget variety of tongs or a smaller version of pincers, pliers or forceps. It is used to grab and remove unwanted things such as excess eyebrow hair, nose-hair, splinters and such. Also convenient for holding small pieces you're trying to glue to other small pieces. Usually unsuccessfully. Some form of a device like tweezers has been found as far back as the Egyptians in 3000 BCE .The word is believed to have evolved from the French word 'etui', pronounced etwee. The verb tweeze is in the dictionary. It is the act of using tweezers.

Wite-out (not in the 1st edition)

There is a product that could have put in the Office category. That is Wite-out. It was invented by Edwin Johanknecht in 1966. He enlisted the help of a friend, George Kloosterhouse who experimented with chemicals. They developed the correction fluid and began to market it. They incorporated in 1971 and registered their trademark "Wite-out" The French company, Societe Bic, yes, Bic, bought the Wite-out company in 1992. Sales decreased significantly after the introduction of word processing programs for personal computers.

There are many other items that weigh less than 16 ounces. Here are some that are not on the list. Should they be? What would you eliminate if you added it?

Adhesive tape	Ash trays	Baby rattles
Balloons	Basters	Batons
Beads	Bells	Bibs
Bolts	Bracelets	Buckles
Bungee cord	Calendar	Chalk
Clothes pins	Coasters	Colander
Comb	Cotton balls	Crayons
Dust pan	Drum sticks	Ear muffs
Extension cord	Fishing net	Flypaper
Gloves	Goggles	Hair brush
Hair curlers	Hair net	Hair spray
Hinges	Hooks	Ice pick
Letter opener	Lotions	Metronome
Money orders	Nail file	Napkins
Ornaments	Pacifier	Padlocks
Staples	Strainer	Sugar packets
Tiddlywinks	Timer (kitchen)	Tinker toys
Tobacco pipe	Waxed paper	

4